saving civility

52 Ways to Tame Rude, Crude & Attitude for a Polite Planet

Sara Hacala

Walking Together, Finding the Way ®
SKYLIGHT PATHS ®
PUBLISHING
Woodstock, Vermont

Saving Civility:
52 Ways to Tame Rude, Crude & Attitude for a Polite Planet

2012 Quality Paperback Edition, Second Printing
© 2011 by Sara Hacala

For information regarding permission to reprint material from this book, please mail or fax your request in writing to SkyLight Paths Publishing, Permissions Department, at the address / fax number listed below, or e-mail your request to permissions@skylightpaths.com.

Library of Congress Cataloging-in-Publication Data
Hacala, Sara, 1949–
  Saving civility : 52 ways to tame rude, crude, and attitude for a polite planet / Sara Hacala. — 2011 quality pbk. ed.
      p. cm.
  Includes bibliographical references (p.   ).
  ISBN 978-1-59473-314-7 (quality pbk.)
  1. Courtesy. 2. Etiquette. I. Title.
  BJ1533.C9H33 2011
  395—dc23
                                                                2011020140

10 9 8 7 6 5 4 3 2
Manufactured in the United States of America
Cover Design: Jenny Buono
Interior Design: Heather Pelham

SkyLight Paths Publishing is creating a place where people of different spiritual traditions come together for challenge and inspiration, a place where we can help each other understand the mystery that lies at the heart of our existence.

SkyLight Paths sees both believers and seekers as a community that increasingly transcends traditional boundaries of religion and denomination—people wanting to learn from each other, *walking together, finding the way.*®

SkyLight Paths, "Walking Together, Finding the Way," and colophon are trademarks of LongHill Partners, Inc., registered in the U.S. Patent and Trademark Office.

Walking Together, Finding the Way®
Published by SkyLight Paths Publishing
A Division of LongHill Partners, Inc.
Sunset Farm Offices, Route 4, P.O. Box 237
Woodstock, VT 05091
Tel: (802) 457-4000   Fax: (802) 457-4004
www.skylightpaths.com

ci·vil·i·ty *n.* Respectful, considerate, and compassionate behavior that enables us to live and work together—locally and globally— embracing our shared humanity and interpersonal connections.

A human being is a part of a whole, called by us the universe, a part limited in time and space. He experiences himself, his thoughts and feelings as something separated from the rest ... a kind of optical delusion of his consciousness. This delusion is a kind of prison for us, restricting us to our personal desires and to affection for a few persons nearest to us. Our task must be to free ourselves from this prison by widening our circle of compassion to embrace all living creatures and the whole of nature in its beauty.

—ALBERT EINSTEIN

⤳ CONTENTS

A Call to Action

The Rise of Rude, Crude, and Attitude

How We're All Part of the Problem

Civility costs nothing and buys everything.
—MARY WORTLEY MONTAGU

We have committed the Golden Rule to memory;
let us now commit it to life.
—EDWIN MARKHAM

As a certified etiquette and protocol consultant, I teach corporate personnel, university students, and youth in at-risk high schools how to communicate respectfully and behave appropriately in business settings so that they can achieve greater success in their lives. I am blessed, for those who seek my expertise already have a vested interest in improving their interactions with others, so that they can develop stronger interpersonal relationships and enhance their professional presence.

What I find alarming is how polite and respectful behavior is vanishing from our world today. We behave and treat one another badly in our day-to-day lives, conduct that causes our relationships and our society at large to fragment and deteriorate, and we are all suffering as a result. Treating people well, and having the crucial ability to develop and maintain meaningful relationships, provides the essential grease that makes our own lives and the rest of the world go round. When that art is lost or missing, we spin out of control into chaos. In a cacophonous sphere, where everyone talks at once but no one listens, where we say hurtful things and do harmful deeds at will without remorse or punishment, and where outrageous exploits are protected by a veil of anonymity, we are fast approaching that danger zone. Without any resistance, bad behavior continues to spread, threatening to become the new normal. Enough is enough. It is time to become uncommonly polite for the common good of all.

While I am not "to the manor born," I grew up in a culture of Southern manners in which we were accustomed to ritualized ways of conveying respect toward one another in our interpersonal relationships. There was a standard of codified behavior that was both accepted and expected. Although we may not have had online social networks back then, word of any misbehavior or lack of compliance with those social codes would have spread to our parents faster than on the Internet, and they would have reprimanded and shamed us into mending our ways. A person's reputation was valued and was always at stake. We were also, by and large, friendly and helpful, and we looked out for one another. Uncommon courtesy was, indeed, very common.

By comparison, I am appalled by and fed up with many of today's free-for-all standards. I am peeved when someone doesn't listen when I speak, continually interrupts our conversation by answering cell phone calls or responding to text messages, stampedes ahead of me in a line, makes tasteless and tactless comments without discretion, or behaves as though he is the only guy on the planet, without any regard for others. I feel angry when a colleague rolls her eyes disparagingly at me, or cuts me off as though my opinion doesn't count.

I am incredulous that *please* and *thank you* are disappearing from our vocabulary. I am distressed when a celebrity who behaves outlandishly in public is idolized as a cultural icon. I am deeply saddened by cruel bullying or invasions of privacy, whether face-to-face or on the Internet, especially when it leaves teenagers feeling so distraught that they believe their only recourse is to take their own lives. I am disgusted by political interactions that are hostile and polarizing, fueled by fevered distortions and mean-spiritedness designed to smear the opposition. I am disturbed that our sense of caring and responsibility is impeded by our own self-absorption.

Perhaps you share my frustration with these types of offenses, which I've dubbed "rude, crude, and attitude." Sadly, rudeness and nastiness are pervasive in our society. Harsh and brash, incivility permeates our interpersonal relationships, the workplace, our schools, and the world at large with devastating effects. There is nothing productive about incivility, and the costs to us—individually, economically, and as a society—are astronomical.

However, it doesn't have to be this way. There are ways that we each can contribute to a polite planet, which is why I have written this book. Your polite and civilized behavior—respectful, thoughtful, kind, inclusive, and generous treatment of others—is not only powerful but also contagious, yielding untold rewards and benefits. Taking a few simple actions described in this book can help you deepen your interpersonal relationships and connections, allowing you to live a life that is ultimately more satisfying. You can make a difference in the lives of others as well as in your community. Moreover, when you treat people with civility, they are more likely to pay this behavior forward to others, creating a planet that is a more enriching and pleasant place to live.

While you may not realize it, you are connected to a great, big universe in which your life powerfully touches the lives of many others. In their extraordinary book *Connected*, Harvard professor and health-care policy specialist Nicholas A. Christakis and University of California, San Diego, political science professor James Fowler analyzed the multiple ways that social networks (not the online variety) shape our voting patterns, happiness, obesity levels, smoking habits, whom we marry, the way we conduct our business, and more. In their findings, Christakis and Fowler determined that "our world is governed by the Three Degrees of Influence Rule: we influence and are influenced by people up to three degrees removed from us, most of whom we do not even know." In experiments subsequent to the book, the duo discovered that acts of generosity contagiously spread among the subjects through the same three levels; conversely, those subjects who experienced stinginess were more likely to pass along the same stingy behavior. Your positive behavior, thus, can effect change in the world with people you don't even know.

Consider how this works. Not surprisingly, most human beings respond positively to respect and kindness; our guard goes down as we soften and begin to trust, relinquishing our resistance to becoming close to others. We're more likely to slow down and be present, to be nicer, and to connect more readily—to others as well as to ourselves. People are attracted to us and want to be in our company. The physiology of our brain and other organs changes. The destructive hormones cortisol and norepinephrine, manufactured by our bodies in times of stress, are held at bay and are replaced by endorphins that make us feel warm and fuzzy. So if we're aware of what makes us feel so good, why don't we open ourselves to more of those opportunities so that we connect more readily with each other?

It goes without saying that this behavior must be heartfelt. Civility is not a hollow or artificial display of proper manners but a mind-set. As the late American journalist and author Mignon McLaughlin once wrote, "Many who would not take the last cookie would take the last lifeboat."

When once the forms of civility are violated, there remains little hope of return to kindness or decency.

—SAMUEL JOHNSON

This introduction describes incivility in our everyday world and the personal and societal toll it exacts. "The Polite Planet Action Guide" consists of fifty-two short chapters that provide solutions so that you, independently, can contribute to making the world a better place to live. Finally, "A Call to Action" is a plea for all of us to join together in our efforts to share this vision, for the common good of all humankind. Above all, this is a book about our *connections* with one another as human beings. It is also about preserving traditions that help those connections flourish. As you read through the following pages, I urge you to look inward, finding your strengths as well as areas that could use some attention. Be willing to ask yourself some tough questions, determining what effort you are willing to make to create a polite planet.

It is not enough simply to *want* the world to be a better place; we have to work at it, with a deep sense of purpose, commitment, courage, and compromise. As in marriage or parenthood, we have to want it badly enough to make the sacrifices and be willing to carry our share of the load.

Each of us has the power to make the planet a more hospitable, pleasant, caring, and safe place to live. This book offers guidelines that go beyond manners and good conduct; it encompasses values and attitudes that help us embrace our shared humanity and connection. It starts with respecting others and recognizing their right to be here. *Saving Civility* is about how we contribute to society and work together—locally and globally—with greater respect, awareness, understanding, and acceptance of one another. A polite planet embodies a worldview of a civilized society—one that is enlightened and empathetic. This is a call to action, an appeal for all of us to be uncommonly polite for the common good of all.

How Rude Can You Be?

Have you ever circled the parking lot of a supermarket, patiently waited with your blinker on for a soon-to-be-vacated space, only to have a car come from another direction and zoom into your spot?

Or perhaps you've been stuck in a checkout line behind someone blasting the airwaves by talking loudly on a cell phone. Not only do you have to listen to details that you'd prefer not to hear, but the continuing conversation interferes with the efficiency of the checkout process, making you wait even longer.

On a highway, a high-speed, aggressive driver assaults you. Bearing down on your bumper, he maneuvers to run you off the road, nearly sideswiping your car.

During a volunteer board meeting, you respectfully present your point of view regarding a controversial issue. A fellow board member disagrees with your position and proceeds to viciously attack you personally, shutting down all discussion.

At the office, an abusive boss unjustly berates and ridicules an employee in front of you and your colleagues. The next day a coworker deliberately excludes you from a meeting, during which he first presents the results of your project but then takes credit for your contribution.

Well, these things don't just happen to you. Recent studies and polls show that there is an upward trend in this country of people who believe that we are not just rude, but that we're becoming increasingly so as compared to the past.

One of the more comprehensive studies, titled "Aggravating Circumstances: A Status Report on Rudeness in America," was conducted by Public Agenda, a public affairs watchdog group, funded by the Pew Charitable Trusts. Although Public Agenda reported some improvements in how we treat others in society, the overall findings showed that 79 percent of our population thought that lack of respect was a serious problem, and that 73 percent believed that we are ruder than we used to be. (It should be noted, however, that 21 percent considered the perception that we are ruder today as merely waxing nostalgic.) Cell-phone usage and mounting road rage were the most often cited incidents, while, generally, rudeness was considered bad for business. Interestingly, 84 percent of adults, including both parents and nonparents, believed that we are no longer teaching our kids manners.

An Associated Press–Ipsos poll reported that 70 percent of the respondents thought that we are ruder today than we were twenty or thirty years ago. Surprisingly, people living in urban areas were thought to be only slightly ruder than those living in rural areas. Again, cell-phone use and road rage were the chief complaints. While stress was considered a major contributing factor, 93 percent of those surveyed in this poll held parents responsible, accusing them of no longer teaching their children manners. Increasingly lax and informal standards were also blamed.

In an ABC News poll, "Rudeness in America," 84 percent of respondents claimed they often or sometimes encountered rude and disrespectful behavior, and 83 percent were bothered by it. At the top of the list of annoying behaviors was—can you guess?—cell-phone abuse, both in public spaces and in interrupting conversations. Bad language was also a big bugaboo.

Following Representative Joe Wilson's outburst, "You lie!" interrupting President Barack Obama's address to Congress in September 2009, a Gallup poll reported that two out of three Americans disapproved of Wilson's behavior. (Six percent were thrilled.) That same month, Rasmussen Reports released the results of a national telephone survey, stating that 75 percent of the respondents felt that Americans are becoming ruder and less civilized. Even more alarming, a June 2011 survey by the public relations firm Weber Shandwick on "Civility in America" reported that the majority of the respondents think that civility will not only continue to decline, but that incivility is the new normal. Further, those polled believe that "incivility in government is perceived to be harming America's future ... and preventing it from moving forward."

Although these studies targeted Americans, the rest of the world is hardly immune to this malady. Over the past two years, I've subscribed to Google Alerts, which notifies me of news and blog articles on rudeness and civility; it appears that bad behavior is a widespread affliction around the globe. Complaints about road rage, desk rage, sports rage, airline rage, cell-phone rage, meeting rage, and just about every other sort of rage are universal. Meanwhile, the call for civility is trumpeted all over.

Whatever Happened to Civility?

Me, me, me, me, me, me, me.

This is not just a vocalizing warm-up but a mantra in an Age of Individualism where our unprecedented penchant for self-expression seemingly has no limits. With social disapproval at an all-time low and only negligible consequences at best, we feel free to say what we want, behave as we want, and dress as we want ... not merely in the privacy of our homes but also in public.

As we embrace informality and laxity, our culture has become increasingly accepting of a standard whereby anything goes. With partisan politics polarizing the country, celebrities behaving badly, and society raging, "rude, crude, and attitude" have never been more in vogue. But over a five-day period in September 2009, three events occurred that rocked the nation:

1. Representative Joe Wilson of South Carolina yelled out, "You lie!" to President Barack Obama as he spoke live in a televised address to Congress.

2. Tennis pro Serena Williams vehemently cursed at a line judge in protest over his call on one of her shots during the U.S. Tennis Open.

3. Rap musician Kanye West crashed the stage at the MTV Video Music Awards, interrupting the acceptance speech of fellow musician Taylor Swift.

Suddenly, boorish and crude behavior was a little less amusing. These brazen incidents, shown on national television, made stunned, and then booing, audiences rise up and finally consider that maybe there are limits to our tolerance for rude behavior, and that perhaps a line had been crossed beyond what is acceptable.

In the weeks and months following these events, the outcry was expressed in hundreds of news articles, editorials (including some in the *New York Times*), and blogs, and across the airwaves. Although denunciation of our lack of manners and civility has been mounting in intensity in recent years (as shown in the news as well as in studies), these particular protests were passionate and ubiquitous. "Whatever happened to civility?" was the hue and cry. In response to those three incidents, however, some quite fairly asked whether there has *ever* been a time when civility truly reigned.

The word *civility* originates from late Middle English, derived from the French *civilité* and from the Latin *civilitas* and *civilis*, "relating to citizens." In its earliest use, the term referred to being a good citizen, with incumbent good behavior, for the good of a community. The "politeness" factor emerged in the sixteenth century.

As time progressed, the context of civility changed in both form and practice. In the Middle Ages, civility was a code that applied only to European royalty and nobility because they were the sole bearers of refinement and culture—people with means as well as the luxury of mobility. Outside of that realm were peasants who neither traveled nor had such prescribed social codes.

Through the centuries, as nations industrialized and commerce expanded, financial opportunity and the means to an education filtered down to an emerging merchant class that developed a sense of urbanity that was certainly below royal stature but above that of the peasants. (The royals, thus, became the first group in history to lament "Whatever happened to civility?" as many of their chivalrous and courtly rules went by the wayside, along with their feudal estates.)

By the nineteenth century, while manners and refined behavior in Europe largely remained the purview of the upper class, they reached a wider audience in the United States. Here, the upper crust attained its stature through the gentrified heritage of ancestors or through accumulated wealth. Those ascending that ladder clamored to become members of a social register, such as Mrs. Astor's 400.

At the same time, thousands of rural folk in America moved far from home to the cities in order to find jobs in factories, joined by an influx of immigrants from abroad, searching for a better life. All these people had journeyed to an unknown place, an environment where nothing was familiar.

As the working class expanded and mobility increased, the need for social and behavioral codes of interaction intensified within these groups of strangers. The rural population wanted to know the ways of the city, and the foreigners sought to become part of their newly adopted land. Ten-cent books on etiquette became a means of providing that structure for these new residents who longed to belong, to be "in the know," and to behave properly, while, gradually, schools assumed the responsibility for teaching manners. Everyone sought to be a "lady" or a "gentleman."

As society has continually evolved, so has the context of specific manners and behaviors, at times causing both confusion and debate over what constitutes correct and incorrect behavior. With increased social interaction across class lines, as well as changing mores, the rules of proper conduct continue to blur. New customs develop while others drop away, resulting in a transformation that inevitably spawns a chorus bemoaning the loss of a long-ago standard that now no longer exists. Thus, the question of "Whatever happened to civility?" has been and will be around for quite a while.

> Life is not so short but that there is always time for courtesy.
>
> —RALPH WALDO EMERSON

Differing Perspectives

So what constitutes "rude" and "uncivilized" conduct today? It is fair to say that not everyone views rude behavior in the same way, which is why, in my seminars, I sometimes do an exercise called, "What is rude to you may not be rude to me." The purpose is for participants to develop an awareness that they may be inadvertently rude to someone and not even know it. For example, I generally don't relish having an unfamiliar person call me by my first name. Some people, however, might respond, "If you call me 'Mr. Brown,' you must be talking about my father!"

Given that participants in my workshops have ranged in age from sixteen to sixty, it is surprising that their individual beliefs about what constitutes disrespect and rude behavior are remarkably similar. Young people complain about texting and cell-phone abuse almost as often as older ones do. No one, it appears, likes to be interrupted, kept waiting, judged as inferior, or ignored. Cutting in line and not taking turns is equally bothersome. People of all ages like to be greeted in return when they say hello, and everyone, it seems, enjoys the undivided attention of others during a conversation. The consensus begins to fray, however, when it comes to dress codes, swearing, and issues involving pop culture.

Admittedly, some rude behaviors are the annoying little grains of sand that are present in all our shoes, making daily life less pleasant. Collectively, however, they amount to a walloping hammer that strikes a blow to us, not just individually, but to society as a whole. And when incivility and disrespect penetrate the workplace, schools, and other public arenas, the toxic aftermath is serious. Residual stress impacts our health, company bottom-line profits erode, classroom learning deteriorates, and forums for respectful, open discussion are closed off. Rudeness incites and incivility bites, while indifference is a death knell.

Rudeness touches every aspect of our lives and gets in the way of our positively connecting with other people. It poisons relationships in our families, in our workplace, and with our friends. It fractures our sense of community. Ultimately, what really matters in the end, however, is not just what we *think* about it, but what we are willing to *do* about it.

So how can we combat the incivility that is eroding our relationships? How can we create a more polite planet, built on respect and responsibility, to pass along to our children?

First, we must understand the causes of our current problem: disconnection, anonymity, increasingly lax standards, and what I call "rabid rhetoric."

The Disconnect

We are living in an unprecedented time and place on this planet. Although change occurs constantly, it is coming at a faster clip than ever before. Our world is getting smaller and more interconnected than we can imagine or keep pace with, transforming our lives exponentially. Nothing, it seems, stays the same, making us feel, at times, powerless and overwhelmed. In our roller-coaster economy, entire industries rise and fall, and jobs come and go in the blink of an eye, adding to our confusion and insecurity about our inability to control much of anything in our lives. At times, a little less change and a little more stability would be welcome.

The effects of these rapid changes put us on shaky ground, making us edgy and uncertain about our future. Daniel Gilbert, professor of psychology at Harvard, cites studies showing that people are more comfortable when they know that something bad *will* occur, rather than suspecting that it *might* occur. Anticipation of what we don't know is more disturbing to us than actually dealing with the aftermath of a negative outcome. Unsure about today, much less tomorrow, we nervously sit and wait.

While we have always lived in an uncertain world, physical distance often allowed us to compartmentalize and separate ourselves from what was happening in a remote location. That began to change during the late 1960s, when televised footage of the Vietnam War entered our living rooms. Now, images from distant lands appear via the Internet within seconds. Further, the ramifications of our global interdependence are becoming increasingly apparent, so that when a small country like Greece threatens to default on its debt, stock markets around the world plummet. Our lives are personally affected. Astonished and confused, we feel disconnected from this unfamiliar new reality, because we no longer know or understand exactly to whom or what we are connecting.

Because our world constantly changes, cultural norms must also continually evolve, as human beings struggle to meet the challenges posed by each subsequent generation. While there are both positive and negative ramifications to these transformations, the inevitable outcome is a greater level of complexity. It is always tempting, therefore, to wax nostalgic about life "in the good old days," since there often seems to be something from the past that we miss and no longer have.

Having grown up in West Virginia in the 1950s, I have my own perspective about what is missing. I was not only taught manners but also very *Southern* manners. "Please," "Thank you," and "Excuse me" were mandatory responses, as well as "Yes ma'am," "No ma'am," "Yes sir," and "No sir." By the age of three, manners had become ingrained.

"Pretty is as pretty does," was my mama's mantra, and, undoubtedly, she made me behave. So when Mama told me to "straighten up and fly right," I obeyed, particularly if I cared about how it might feel to sit down again. My upbringing was not an anomaly, however: This kind of manners was expected behavior among all children I knew, both at home and in public—especially in school. We were also immensely respectful of authority figures in our lives, notably teachers, whose rules we regarded in much the same way as we did those of our parents. There were consequences if we did not comply, and our misbehavior was punishable without a teacher being fearful of reproach from parents.

Adults were also exceedingly polite to one another. You might question the merit and sincerity of these manners, considering that the South, however polite, was also a place where people were hanged from trees, their only crime being the color of their skin. Unquestionably, the history of that legacy cannot be disavowed. I am proud to say, notwithstanding, that I lived during the time of *Brown v. Board of Education of Topeka*, and that, as a result of that 1954 landmark Supreme Court decision, West Virginia was the first state in the country to integrate the races in public schools, when that became the new law of the land.

That said, life was indeed slower than it is today, though still complex. In 1957, three years after the *Brown* decision, we were caught up in a scientific race with the Soviets after the launch of their satellite, Sputnik. Shortly thereafter, we were practicing drills in our classrooms, diving under our desks in the event of a nuclear attack. Obviously, the simplicity of a *Leave It to Beaver* world has never existed in reality. However, our day-to-day living five decades ago did not feel as stressful as life does today, and we were a lot kinder and more pleasant to one another.

We *took time* to talk, visit, and connect with people—whether it was a conversation in the grocery store, with a neighbor over a backyard fence, or in someone's kitchen over a cup of coffee—all part of our daily lives. Visits were often spontaneous, with friends or relatives popping in.

Children's lives were largely unscheduled. In my neighborhood, we just showed up and played. Kids from three to fourteen would emerge from their houses; meet up in someone's backyard; and play tag, hide-and-seek, and Red Rover. We rode bikes and didn't come home until we were called for dinner. Like our parents, we got together often, face-to-face—a big contrast to today's prearranged playdates slotted weeks in advance.

All that has changed, even in West Virginia, where life is still only a little slower than in some parts of the country. We're frantic over our work, deadlines, shuttling our overscheduled kids from one activity to another, multitasking, and worrying about our health, our bills, and how we are going to send our kids to college, retire, and survive.

And the kids resemble their pressured parents, becoming increasingly stressed out and anxious. As colleges raise their entrance requirements, the competition for grades, test scores, and developing a résumé full of extracurricular activities often begins in elementary school, and, within some families, before nursery school. With their harried schedules, young people take multitasking to a new level, using all the technological tools at their disposal, texting and simultaneously contacting hundreds of people on social media sites with a few deft keystrokes.

For both adults and kids, overscheduling, the frenetic pace of daily life, and the way we communicate have led to a disconnect—a lack of time and care for the personal relationships that bind us together as a society.

Technologically Speaking

One of the culprits behind this disconnect is, undoubtedly, the very technology that has catapulted us forward economically and culturally. Historically, advancements in transportation and technology have broadened our reach and narrowed the distance between communities. Roads, canals, ships, railroads, cars, and airplanes have progressively expanded our exploration of the world and the speed at which people and goods travel. The printing press, the telegraph, the telephone, radio, television, and the Internet have provided increasingly efficient channels for disseminating information.

Yet these developments have had a somewhat paradoxical effect on society in terms of human connection: While our mobility in the world may have been extended, we haven't necessarily become closer as people. Traveling to unfamiliar locales does expose us to new places and does put us in contact with a larger population, but these may be people we don't know and with whom we will never share any sort of connection.

The mounting volume of information to which we have access has grown at such an exponential rate that, inundated, we find ourselves dog-paddling in an ever-widening sea of data. As a result, the fraction of information that we can possibly consume, compared to that which is available, becomes increasingly smaller, at times making us feel smaller and overwhelmed—yet another disconnect.

As advertisers seek to expand their penetration into online and social media markets, they bombard us with messages from every conceivable direction. Up-to-the-second news is reported from multiple sources and delivered via multiple channels, from Yahoo! to Google Alerts to RSS feeds, not to mention conventional broadcast and print media, which also maintain their own online presence. You know what your best friend is doing every minute because of her timely tweets and social media posts. Every corporation, organization, retailer, and political candidate has not only a website but also a Facebook fan page. Chances are that your favorite author, as well as anyone else you may know, is among the 133 million bloggers worldwide registered by Technorati. Most of these bloggers' articles are open for comment, as are chat rooms for every conceivable topic. By spring 2010, shared user-generated content—web links, news stories, blog posts, photos, and so forth—amounted to 305 billion pieces per week on Facebook alone.

In addition to the amount of information it provides, the Internet has created a tectonic shift in the speed and manner with which we communicate. We talk to people, not so much face-to-face or even voice-to-voice, but via small screens. Geographical distance is of no consequence: Our messages flow around the globe but also from room to room, at lightning speed, via orbiting satellites thousands of miles high in the sky.

> There is more to life
> than simply
> increasing its speed.
>
> —MOHANDAS GANDHI

We are in instant and constant contact through ubiquitous e-mails, texts, and other forms of computer messaging. We forward copious e-mails to groups of friends and families as our way of "staying in touch." We use social media pages to inform people about our lives or comment on those of others. Condolence messages are sent via Twitter. Multitasking with multimedia is the new norm. While technology has created more avenues to contact more people, it is a style of communication that is decidedly *less personal*.

There's less time to pick up the phone and talk or meet in person, because our lives are so busy, not only with the matters of day-to-day living, but also in dealing with hundreds of e-mails and urgent texts. When we do talk, it is frequently on a cell phone in a public arena, without notice of or sensitivity to those around us, causing disruption and annoyance.

If there's any doubt as to the pervasiveness of Internet communication and text messaging, consider the facts. The Pew Research Center reported that, in the United States, as of December 2009, 74 percent of adults used the Internet, with 71 percent of those connected on a daily basis; further, 58 percent used e-mail regularly and 27 percent were members of a social media network. Nielsen statistics showed that the growth of social media networking was up 82 percent globally in 2009 over the previous year. Overall, the average user spent fifty-eight hours per month on the Internet.

The Radicati Group in Palo Alto, which provides research on Internet and wireless technologies, estimated in 2009 that there were 1.4 billion global e-mail users who sent 247 billion messages every day, amounting to over 90 trillion in 2009. That same source predicts that by 2013, the number of users will grow to 1.9 billion, who are expected to send 507 billion e-mails.

Although in 2009 the *Wall Street Journal* forecasted a decline in the use of e-mail, other sources indicate an opposite trend. The Radicati Group predicts that businesspeople worldwide will send and receive an average of 219 e-mails per day in 2013, compared to 167 in 2009. And e-mails don't have to be accessed by way of a conventional computer; Radicati reports that, globally, there were 139 million mobile e-mails sent in 2009, a figure that is expected to grow to more than one billion in 2013. Those multipurpose phones also provide the means to text. The International Association for the Wireless Communications Industry (CTIA) reported that there were 292 million wireless customers in 2010 that sent roughly 900 billion texts in the first half of that year; 6.4 billion text minutes accrue per day. The Pew Research Center released a report in April 2010, stating that 75 percent of twelve- to seventeen-year-olds had cell phones, and that one in three of those teens sent more than one hundred text messages per day.

While these statistics may seem staggering, they point to the fact that our incessant, frenetic, and constant contact via small screens and a few buttons feeds our modern-day obsession with instant gratification. However, these are often immediate communications without time for thought or reflection.

Constant contact is not the same as connection. That is not to say that Internet communication is necessarily a harmful or destructive force in our lives; in fact, we cannot imagine how we would manage without it, nor would we want to. Nonetheless, when our personal interaction is not balanced with human face-to-face or even voice-to-voice contact, we become increasingly disconnected and isolated from one another. With MP3 players growing out of our ears and our eyes glued to screens, we are further distracted and "hermetically sealed," often failing to see the people physically standing before us.

It is fair to say, however, that the Internet has not only altered our style of communication, but it is also altering our concept of what community means. Whereas we once thought of community as a group of people living and interacting together in a physical space, community can now be virtual—amorphous and abstract—although, to some, no less real. People who never meet one another face-to-face develop bonds based on common interests, communicated via blogging sites. Social media networks offer an expansive platform whereby the most intimate details of a person's life can be delivered to a limitless audience.

As change occurs, society evolves and new cultural norms develop, and, undoubtedly, the Internet has opened new possibilities for efficient contact with others and access to information. So powerful are the Internet and social media networks in galvanizing public opinion that they play a major strategic role in election and advertising campaigns; they have also been a critical component in the downfall of tyrannical political regimes. Nonetheless, it remains a more impersonal form of communication, and if we rely on it exclusively, we risk disconnecting ourselves from close, meaningful interpersonal relationships.

The Anonymity Factor

Once, in the parking lot of a supermarket, I witnessed a young man who deliberately, with a slight shove, allowed his empty shopping cart to roll into the door of a parked vehicle. Aghast and speechless, I finally managed a remonstrative "What are you doing?" Flippantly, he retorted, "What do I care? It's not my car!" Miraculously, there was no damage—I was poised to summon the police or initiate a citizen's arrest.

Such conduct makes us wonder not only what has happened in this person's life to make him behave in this manner but also what has happened to our society today when the behavior of so many is out of control. Stephen L. Carter, professor of law at Yale and author of *Civility: Manners, Morals, and the Etiquette of Democracy*, proposes that social approval is not as important as it used to be. He writes, "A big part of our incivility crisis stems from the sad fact that we do not know each other or even want to try; and, not knowing each other, we seem to think that how we treat each other does not matter."

Anonymity, thus, can be a big factor in our rudeness. When we don't know the people around us, we feel free to do anything that we want. It becomes easy to get away with misbehavior when there is little chance of seeing that person again.

Stanford University emeritus professor of psychology Philip Zimbardo, known primarily for his work on the psychology of evil, decries the malicious consequences of anonymity, whether it is introduced as a factor in controlled laboratory experiments or evidenced within the general population. Numerous studies, according to Zimbardo, show how human beings, when disguised or otherwise unrecognizable, can be coaxed into performing outrageous acts, behavior they might not otherwise engage in. Outside of the scientific laboratory, we at times witness unspeakable misbehavior, which threatens to become a new normal, largely fueled and protected by the veil of anonymity. Think cyberbullying. Think stalking. Think road rage. Think the Ku Klux Klan. Anonymity may serve a useful purpose for spies, but it is a scourge against any efforts toward building a cohesive, civilized community.

Living anonymously is a fact that we've come to expect in large cities, as the sheer numbers of people make it impossible for us to become personally involved in the affairs of everyone; otherwise, we'd be overwhelmed. However, today's rushed, high-pressure lifestyles also serve to insulate and isolate us, creating a buffer that simulates anonymity, resulting in less personal interaction, even in small towns.

As a result, we stop exchanging small pleasantries with one another and fail to perform random acts of kindness. When someone is generous to us, we often don't even have the courtesy to nod or express gratitude. When we do talk, we are often brief and abrupt, as we are anxious to get on to the next item on our agenda.

By avoiding eye contact—often as we focus on cell-phone conversations, texting, or MP3 players—we cease to see people in our midst, looking over their heads or through them as if they were pieces of cellophane. Absorbed in our own thoughts and agendas, we climb over people like imaginary stairs, rendering them invisible, as though they don't exist. We become so unaware of what is happening directly around us that we fail to notice that an elderly man or pregnant woman on the bus could benefit from the seat that we happen to be occupying. While our outward behavior may not be intentionally rude, our self-created barriers permit us to live in our own little worlds, apart from those around us.

In this respect, anonymity is a self-imposed lifestyle choice that impairs connection with others and restricts a sense of belonging. Make no mistake, however: that anonymity can also be an aggressive and brutal weapon. A few years ago, the school superintendent in our town of nine thousand residents came under vitriolic attack for an impropriety that she had perpetrated in her previous position in another district. Much of the criticism came in the form of unsigned letters to the editor of our local newspaper, which provided a platform for expression with impunity. Following the superintendent's subsequent suicide, the editorial policy of the paper was changed, prohibiting the publication of anonymous letters, leaving our town to debate, in the words of the *New York Times*, "where fair comment ends and schoolhouse bullying begins."

Anonymity provides a wide berth and a platform for rampant rudeness on the Internet, where people can be whoever they want to be or say anything they please with few constraints. While some blogs filter inappropriate comments, there are plenty of other platforms that operate without restriction, an arena that allows equal opportunity for all subject matter. Instant and widespread messaging provides a sweeping forum for spreading malicious gossip, rumors, and falsehoods. In some instances, cyberbullying has become so vicious that some teenagers who have been so victimized have killed themselves.

Again, the Internet is merely a tool for dissemination and access—faster and more penetrating than a speeding bullet. It's how we use it that matters.

"It's the Mud, Stupid"

It's not only technology that is stretching the fragile connections between us all. Our society is becoming increasingly fragmented by polarized politics and media, making it difficult for us to listen and relate to one another.

Although many of us, myself included, carp at the ongoing negativism and distortion that each new season of political campaigning brings, historians are quick to point out episodes from our past that are far more outrageous than what goes on now. A case in point is the election of 1828 when General Andrew Jackson was referred to as a murderer and his wife as a whore. Furthermore, history records the outrageous caning of prominent abolitionist Senator Charles Sumner of Massachusetts, on May 22, 1856, by pro-slavery Congressman Preston Brooks of South Carolina on the floor of the U.S. Senate. It took more than three years for Sumner to recover from his injuries and return to his post.

However, while our political past is rife with episodes ranging from overt disrespect to outright violence, today we only have to turn on our "news" program of choice to witness daily acts of incivility. Consider the unwieldy maelstrom of town hall meetings, forums in which to air and debate controversial topics. Regrettably, whether it is the media coverage or an actual event, what often takes place is not "straight talk" on the issues themselves. Instead, rabid rhetoric—full of distortion, personal attacks, and political ideology—takes over so that the outcome is polarizing paralysis, not solutions.

The media amplifies much of this extremist political antagonism with exclamatory and inflammatory "talking heads" who serve as hosts of ersatz news programs that are little more than biased infomercials for a particular point of view. Take your pick: You can find a program on a twenty-four-hour news channel that supports your belief. Those broadcasts, however, are more self-serving than many viewers realize: Their ultimate goal is to win a ratings contest; the more viewers a program has, the more revenue it can generate from advertising dollars. Thus, many of the stories are hyped and hot, dumbing us down and rendering us intellectually flabby.

In order for this formula to work, however, there have to be clamoring buyers. If we don't buy, the media doesn't sell. Therefore, it is *we* who create our media culture, not the other way around; we are in control. And it is always our prerogative to turn off the television, to refuse to buy a newspaper, to shun an Internet site. As Os Guinness writes in *A Case for Civility: And Why Our Future Depends on It*, "Moderates ... have no mailing lists. Clean campaigns lose. Conflict sells. The best ads are the worst ads. It's the mud, stupid."

Richard A. Posner, Federal Circuit Court judge and author of numerous books on economics, suggests that the mainstream media, already liberal, has been pushed even further to the left by the rise of the new media, which is more of an economic than a political phenomenon. As a result, there is greater polarization in the reporting. In a highly competitive news market, as more newcomers burst onto the scene, there is an increasingly intense struggle for an audience, creating an arena in which to cater to what the consumer wants. One way to accomplish this is to create a niche market for a sector not previously served. Another, states the *New York Times*, "is to 'shout louder' than the competitors, where shouting takes the form of a sensational attention-grabbing discovery, accusation, claim or photograph."

A paper by Shanto Iyengar and Kyu Hahn titled "Red Media, Blue Media: Evidence of Ideological Polarization in Media Use," prepared for the annual meeting of the International Communication Association by the Political Communication Lab at Stanford University, credited the emergence of Fox News as contributing to the polarization of the news audience. But no matter which way you lean, according to the report, "exposure to one-sided news coverage is an 'echo chamber' effect—the news serves to reinforce existing beliefs and attitudes."

Not limited to television, fanatical extremism is also prevalent on radio, the Internet, and in the print media. This phenomenon is not new: Yellow journalism has used sensationalism to sell newspapers for more than a hundred years. Growing competition produces greater fragmentation among the news sources, with each doing what it can to capture the consumer. Thus, in this sort of environment, there will always be more vocally radical points of view, propelling the media toward greater polarization.

With diminishing restrictions and expanding latitude, we are continually pushing the envelope with entertainment media as well. During the Golden Age of Hollywood, married couples were depicted as sleeping in twin beds, a tradition that has not been observed since before 1960. Censors were powerful in their influence as to what was acceptable on a movie or television screen and what was not. Swearing was avoided, which is why movie audiences were rocked when Clark Gable uttered one of the most famous lines on celluloid: "Frankly, my dear, I don't give a damn." It has only been in recent years that most curse words were not totally bleeped from television broadcasts.

Fast-forward to today, where our lust for sensationalism has created an edgier culture, whereby it takes increasing levels of shock to grab our attention and hold our interest. Anything goes as long as it sells. We are inundated with depictions of vulgarity, foul language, graphic sex, nudity, and violence in all media as well as in areas of our own lives. Where we once had *I Love Lucy* and *Father Knows Best*, we now have reality television with cast members eating cockroaches and swapping wives. As viewers and listeners become inured, the "shock" becomes mainstream, until a more thrilling lure attracts us.

Our values are also reflected in the celebrities we choose to worship and admire. On any given day, observe the top ten searches on an Internet search engine. There's usually an obnoxious and out-of-control celebrity on the list whose antics we're eager to follow. Whether living vicariously or simply absorbed as voyeurs, we feel entitled to know the most intimate details of the lives of people we neither know nor share any real connection to other than through their public visibility.

No Butts about It

Dress codes are another prime example in our shift toward informality and laxity. While fashion trends change constantly, an adherence to a certain standard of dress remained much the same for centuries until recently. You wore a tie to the office, a Sunday dress to church, and formal attire to a ball. Different occasions called for specific clothing, and society, for the most part, complied.

Today, however, quite frequently anything goes. Some clothing styles often leave nothing to the imagination, and are offensive to many, creating rifts between generations and cultures. Low-slung pants that expose butt cracks, bra-sized tank tops that reveal breasts and midriffs, and skimpy skirts are worn everywhere—to school, to religious services, on a job interview. And when the Girls' 2005 Championship Lacrosse Team at Northwestern University was invited to the Rose Garden by President Bush, they wore flip-flops, creating a media sensation.

There is often resistance to the rigidity of dress codes because these standards interfere with self-expression. However, self-expression sometimes needs to be put on the back burner as a sign of respect, which is, fundamentally, what dress codes are all about. A grandmother once confided to me that she was ashamed of her grandson when he came to a wake at a funeral home wearing baggy pants that hung from the lower edge of his bottom. On one hand, she was pleased that he had taken the time to show up and pay his respects; however, she was mortified that he had done so disrespectfully.

In these two examples, it's probably not just a matter of choice that is at stake, but also a lack of awareness. Our standards have become so loose and lax and our expression so unrestrained that some people have no idea that they themselves are even considered rude by others.

Rude or Edgy?

Not everyone agrees that we are ruder today than in the past or that our incivility is a more frequent occurrence, but that we simply have more ways to
get the message out. With the Internet, we are not restricted to conventional
means of communication; we're able to access and view something repeatedly and also pass it on to our friends, creating an even larger audience.

I agree with this supposition, but only to a point. We, indeed, have
greater exposure than before. The content of those messages, however, is
far more shocking than it was even a few years ago, often propelling vulgarity and sensationalism to its outer limits.

Our rude behavior—on the Internet or in person—is divisive and
pushes people away, creating a further disconnect in the wake of bruised
or angry feelings. It will be a pity if our current rudeness becomes a cultural norm, for it is a legacy that will be passed along to future generations.
We have an opportunity to reverse course, which first requires us to take
a long and honest look at ourselves, becoming aware of our behavior and
how we treat others. In order to connect with people, we must *slow down*
and take the time to develop those relationships; otherwise, we miss out
on the best opportunities of our lives.

Incivility Bites

Incivility takes many different forms across all segments of our society.
What one person determines to be uncivil, or not, can be highly subjective. Most would agree that bullying or physically assaulting a person is a
destructive act. However, there are subtler yet equally insidious forms of
intimidation and disrespect, intended to discredit or undermine another
person, that are sometimes more tricky to pinpoint as incivility and that
often fly below the radar. There are two arenas in which incivility is literally and figuratively costing us dearly: the office and the classroom.

The Bad Business of Incivility

After studying the effects of incivility in the workplace and collecting data
for more than a decade, business management school professors Christine
Pearson and Christine Porath documented their findings in an invaluable

book, *The Cost of Bad Behavior: How Incivility Is Damaging Your Business and What to Do about It*. In their book, they explore the harmful ramifications of incivility, which they define as "the exchange of seemingly inconsequential inconsiderate words and deeds that violate conventional norms of workplace conduct."

Because some acts of rudeness and discourtesy appear less blatant than outright physical violence, they can be open to interpretation. For example, a coworker who doesn't say hello, leaves a snippy voice-mail message, or neglects to say please or thank you may not bother one person but may deeply offend another. Such acts, however, can be intentional forms of covert aggression. The authors list twenty-four such uncivil behaviors that also include spreading false rumors, sabotaging an individual's project or taking credit for it, withholding information, excluding someone from a meeting, and throwing temper tantrums. Reflective of our larger rude culture, these behaviors are pervasive in the workplace: According to Pearson and Porath, 96 percent of employees have experienced incivility on the job. Whether flagrant or disguised, incivility results in enormous costs that are far from inconsequential.

In *The No Asshole Rule: Building a Civilized Workplace and Surviving One That Isn't*, Robert I. Sutton, professor of management science and engineering at Stanford University, has his own list of what constitutes "asshole behavior." His simple test for determining who falls into this category involves two criteria. One, does the target, after talking to the alleged perpetrator, feel worse about himself? Two, does the alleged perpetrator generally target people who are not powerful more often than those who are? While the answer to the first question is somewhat subjective, Sutton also points to a multitude of studies worldwide that show that nastiness, bullying, and a culture of fear in the workplace are costly, in terms of morale, emotional health, and loss of dollars.

According to Sutton, other studies show that negative behavior has five times greater impact than positive behavior, in that it is felt more deeply. Worse, it is viral: Negative conduct poisons the culture of a workplace, in large part because it is so contagious. As it spreads, Sutton says, more people behave badly themselves.

Stress—the leading cause of worker disability—promotes increased rudeness and incivility and also triggers a range of spiraling negative emotions.

Pearson and Porath report that stress costs the American economy $300 billion annually and that the cost of treating stress-related illnesses amounts to $200 billion globally. When a company downsizes, with fewer employees to shoulder the same work, stress frequently skyrockets.

Losses to a company's bottom line caused by incivility are *calculable*, say Pearson and Porath, as they are tied to:

- Lower productivity
- Reduced commitment
- Lack of motivation
- Employees offering fewer suggestions
- Greater absenteeism, tardiness, and long-term disability
- More managerial time spent dealing with employee conflicts
- Employee replacement costs, which can amount to four times a worker's annual salary
- Less-effective teamwork

Additionally, lack of job security today engenders a lack of loyalty, on the part of both the company and its employees, which impacts the quality of relationships. Pearson and Porath's research reveals that one in eight employees will leave a job due to an incident of incivility, and that of one million workers polled by Gallup in 2007, problems with immediate supervisors were the most common reason for changing jobs.

Other losses are harder to calculate, but no less real. When employees leave, they not only take their experience and knowledge with them, but they also can cause further damage to the reputation of a business by talking to other people, including customers. While still on the job, disgruntled workers may even express their frustration by being disrespectful, discourteous, and otherwise unresponsive to customers, provoking those customers to simply walk away, resulting in an incalculable loss of income for firms. For example, a waiter with an attitude may repel customers, and turn tables less frequently. (In that scenario, unfortunately, the waiter also loses and, thus, "turns the table" against himself.) The old adage that it is cheaper to retain an old customer than develop a new one is not just an axiom; it is a statistically proven fact.

In his book *Satisfied Customers Tell Three Friends, Angry Customers Tell 3,000*, Pete Blackshaw writes about consumer-generated media (CGM), whereby a complaint from even a single displeased customer can be carried to millions of readers. Further, he refers to companies with great products and services that lose business every day due to poor customer service.

Not only do customers resent being treated badly themselves, they also are negatively affected when they witness employers treating their employees badly in public. Whether you are a customer, a coworker, or an innocent bystander, Pearson and Porath point to numerous studies that report that observing the public abuse of an employee by an employer is almost as harmful and threatening as being the actual target yourself.

Although there is no work environment where incivility is pleasant, in the medical community, it can be deadly. Bullying staff—particularly nurses by doctors and/or by other nurses—can have seriously harmful consequences, affecting patient safety and welfare. Sutton refers to a study by Amy Edmonson, funded by Harvard Medical School physicians, which ironically showed that nursing units with the best leaders reported making ten times as many mistakes as those with the worst leaders. Further investigation revealed that the nurses with the best leaders reported their mistakes more frequently because they felt "psychologically safe" within their units and were "never afraid to tell the nurse manager." By contrast, nurses who seldom reported errors worked in units where there was an unforgiving climate of fear, so they hid mistakes from their supervisors.

While errors in medicine are common, the way they are *handled* can make all the difference in their outcome. Columbia University School of Law professor William H. Simon has written about an experiment at the Veterans' Affairs Medical Center in Lexington, Kentucky. A new policy required staff members to disclose all mistakes and apologize to the patient or his family; further, they also recommended legal counsel, immediately providing all relevant records. The supposition was that suits are motivated more often by mistrust and anger than by financial incentives.

The experiment proved to be successful, and the transparency of the medical center's policy had its own rewards. For although the number of claims increased, due to information the patients previously may not have known, the cost of the claims went down. Apologies helped assuage bad feelings, and the policy, overall, provided an open platform for corrective measures and improvements to be made.

In *Blink*, author Malcolm Gladwell relates a study conducted by University of Toronto professor of medicine Wendy Levinson. A foremost researcher on physician-patient communication, Levinson questioned why some doctors, though highly skilled, were often sued while others, who made many mistakes, never faced a medical malpractice suit. The results showed that the surgeons who showed their concern by spending an average of three minutes longer with each patient were not sued. "But in the end," Gladwell adds, "it comes down to a matter of respect, and the simplest way that respect is communicated is through tone of voice, and the most corrosive tone of voice that a doctor can assume is a dominant tone." Civility goes a long way, therefore, in alleviating the deleterious effects of mistrust and anger.

In *Leading with Kindness*, authors William Baker and Michael O'Malley cite six elements underlying kindness in the workplace: compassion, integrity, gratitude, authenticity, humility, and humor. Their premise is that a kind work environment encourages problem solving and resilience, and promotes growth and creativity.

The Generational Divide

These days, however, incivility occurs not just between individuals; it frequently threads along generational lines, spurred by as many as three, and sometimes four, age groups working side by side in the same space. Differences in perceived values, communication styles, and approaches to solving problems have created so many tensions between older and younger workers that an entire industry of consultants has been spawned to provide solutions for this corporate dilemma.

Every generation has been shaped by the events of its time. The Great Depression and World War II influenced the "matures" or "GI traditionalists," those born between 1925 and 1945. Although the baby boomers were born during a period of overall economic stability and prosperity (1946–1964), they were also impacted by the assassinations of public figures as well as the national political unrest and upheaval marked by the Vietnam War and Watergate. The rise of feminism, increased divorce rates, working moms, and the beginnings of computer-age technology (video games) during 1965 to 1979 were all factors that influenced generation X, often referred to as the "latchkey" kids. Largely characterized by their independence, members of this group were also affected by economic shifts and reversals, such as the dot-com bust.

Members of generation Y, the youngest in today's workforce, were born roughly between 1980 and the mid-1990s. Also known as the millennials, the Internet generation, and the echo boomers, they have grown up in a digital age of unparalleled technological advances in communication, making them the most computer-savvy and tech-oriented people on the planet. In addition, they grew up in a child-centered environment, raised by parents whose constant praise, encouragement, and attention led them to believe that there was little that they could not do; even the most modest of accomplishments won applause.

These varying influential events and circumstances have created a wide spectrum of workers who possess highly divergent views, attitudes, and expectations regarding on-the-job performance and behavior. Common areas of friction center around differing perceptions of work ethic, organizational hierarchy, dealing with change, and technology issues. According to a 2004 Society for Human Resource Management study, nearly half of its members were grappling with intergenerational conflict. A survey conducted by PricewaterhouseCoopers, published in 2009, reported that 61 percent of chief executives from forty-four countries said that they had problems assimilating younger workers into their companies.

To baby boomers and older members of generation X, members of generation Y often seem to reflect a sense of entitlement, impatience, and not wanting to pay their dues. They are seen as having fewer interpersonal skills, important in building relationships. Older workers often view Ys as clueless as to what constitutes a respectful code of conduct on the job, including appropriate dress. Informal and overly familiar, Ys are not bashful about addressing senior executives by their first names or even asking a CEO for a ride home.

Members of generation Y, with their fluid technological skills and ability to multitask, however, have their own criticisms of their older counterparts. Because they have often worked together in groups in school, they sometimes have a leg up in terms of collaboration and team-building. They've had more exposure to the concept that "there is more than one right answer," which, when combined with technological solutions, can make them fresh and innovative thinkers. As a result, Ys become impatient with traditionalists, whom they view as narrowly focused, staid, stodgy, and unwilling to change because "we've always done it this way." Further, having grown up in a world that is increasingly global and multicultural, the Ys are more accepting of gender, racial, sexual, and ethnic diversity— acceptance that they sometimes find lacking in their older colleagues.

Unquestionably, misunderstandings often arise between younger and older workers; however, they are sometimes based on myths that can be debunked. Whatever the resentments, the big picture indicates that workers of multiple generations will be working side by side for many years to come. The millennials are also by far the largest generation of workers ever to emerge, so they represent now *and* the future. Further, we are all living in a digital age, which is shaping the way that we do business.

Rather than arguing with one another, it is crucial to find ways to understand one another and get along, but also to *collaborate*. So whether my audience is older or younger, my advice is remarkably similar. In order for harmonious, workable, and productive relationships to flourish, each side needs to bend, casting aside preconceived judgments, and find a way to learn and value the other's background and abilities. Boomers have been building companies' bottom lines, relying on their knowledge and the strength of their interpersonal relationships, for more years than gen Y has been alive. Older audiences can avail themselves of the vast technological skills and innovative thinking that Ys can offer. An engineer from an aviation company once told me about a new recruit who, the first day on the job, came up with an alternative idea for a more efficient assembly of a wheel structure that ultimately saved the corporation millions of dollars. Research is bearing out that, because of their exposure to technology at such a young age, the brains of the millennials are actually developing differently than those of older generations. Average IQ scores are also increasing by three points each decade. Therefore, there is a lot of collective brainpower that can be tapped.

Respectful communication is absolutely vital, which means *listening* and really *hearing* what each of us has to say. That means that no eye-rolling, sneering, contempt, malicious gossiping, sarcasm, belittling, withholding of information, exclusion, or other divisive, uncivil behaviors are allowed. Good manners are always appropriate and provide an effective way to build bridges.

An Uncivil Education

Businesses aren't the only institutions paying a high price for bad behavior. Disrespect in our schools is a gargantuan issue that undermines the quality of learning in our classrooms. For decades, schools have dealt with the challenges of disruptive behavior in differing ways, whether adopting codes of conduct or implementing various means of character education. In 2005, for example, the Bronx Public Schools initiated a pilot program teaching etiquette, contending that students who were better behaved would become better learners. What is unexpected, however, is the erosion of behavioral standards in college classrooms, where some professors report that students openly address them with foul language or walk out of class in the middle of a lecture.

Administrators and teachers often have a tough row to hoe these days, maintaining behavioral standards and upholding civility codes, even in the best schools. Fearing parents who threaten litigation, our educators today are constrained from imposing almost any sort of discipline. The irony, however, is that while we often take teachers to task for trying to instill the lessons we should be teaching at home, we hold the schools responsible for the way our kids behave.

During a talk I once gave on civility, a woman insisted that it was actually the role of the schools to teach table manners since her kids' sports schedules prevented her family from having dinner together. She believed that she could not be expected to be the manners coach or police. My suggestion that she find one meal a week for this instruction was rebuffed. I didn't argue, but, frankly, those manners should have been taught years ago. Teaching and modeling manners begins at home, long before kids go to school or pick up a bat, ball, or racket. They need to learn that other people's feelings matter, not just their own.

With amazement, I've observed kids running around like holy terrors without supervision, flinging food on the floor in restaurants, treating the waitstaff like personal servants, abusively talking back to their parents, and throwing tantrums at the mall without a word of admonishment. What are these parents *thinking*? A child doesn't outgrow bad behavior; it only gets worse, with many unfortunate consequences later in life.

Personally, in our household, my husband was by far the more lenient parent; he often fell prey to the spells of our young daughter's charms and looked the other way when she misbehaved. Willing to play the "heavy," more than once I cautioned, "Don't raise a kid that only *you* can stand!" Unquestionably, our daughter Katie was given unconditional love, but also structure, limits, and boundaries; growing up, she learned that her actions had consequences. She was permitted to express herself openly as long as she did so respectfully and appropriately. We treated her with the utmost respect but also insisted that we had the right to expect the same in return. Although we assured her that nothing would ever diminish our love for her, we also made it clear that any lack of respect would undermine our relationship.

While our own children may be the center of *our* lives, they need to be taught at an early age that they share the planet with other people with whom they need to get along, beginning with their nuclear families. If our kids don't practice manners, behave appropriately, and interact well in social situations at home, they can't be expected to take what they haven't been taught out into the world. They cannot become model citizens if no one has modeled that behavior for them, held them to a higher standard, or taught them the right thing to do. Neither can they build respectful and successful interpersonal relationships in their future careers if they haven't learned to connect with and develop an awareness of other people, long before they seek a job.

We have already glimpsed the culture clash between older and younger generations in the workplace. From my own perspective as a consultant, I can vouch that the millennials (or members of *any* age group) who hit the marketplace equipped with a professional demeanor, appropriate social skills, and an ability to relate to and get along with their fellow workers—young and old—have a competitive advantage and increased marketability. As Theodore Roosevelt stated a hundred years ago, "The most important ingredient in the formula of success is knowing how to get along with people."

Civilly Speaking

The statistics and examples discussed here make the case that rudeness is rampant, possibly even epidemic, in our society. Sadly, it is more than annoying behavior at stake; lack of consideration for others can lead to lost business, problems at home and in school, and fractured relationships. At its worst, volatile anger and uncontrolled emotions can prompt violence, sometimes resulting in serious injury or death. But for now, let's say that not every incident of rudeness is life-threatening. Does that fact make it any less, well, aggravating? The important issue here is how rudeness makes someone feel.

Only you can determine the effect that uncivil behavior has on you. Does it make your blood boil when someone cuts in front of you, or are you able to brush off annoyances like that? Does it irritate you when people take cellphone calls or text during a meeting or a movie, or are you becoming inured to such interruptions, accepting this behavior as life in the twenty-first century? Does it bother you to be treated as though you were invisible? If your feelings are hurt by unkindness, do you let those emotions slide or do you carry them around for hours or days? Does the rude behavior of others make you feel closer to them or does it make you don a suit of armor in order to withstand the slings and arrows directed your way?

Lastly, do you see rude people only as "them," or is it ever you? Unfortunately, we don't always see ourselves as we really are, nor are we always willing to admit our mistakes. While it is possible that some of us may be rude all of the time, we must acknowledge that all of us are probably rude some of the time. As Walt Kelly, creator of the comic strip *Pogo*, had his eponymous character observe, "We have met the enemy, and he is us."

Happily, with a little dedicated effort, there *are* things that we can do to elevate our own behavior and, hopefully, inspire others to do the same. In the next part of the book, we will explore fifty-two "Polite Planet Actions," each comprising proactive measures that you as an individual can take, enabling you to connect more positively and respectfully and communicate better with the people around you, and that will benefit your community at large. You may note that the phrase "ripple effect" is used repeatedly, becoming a theme of this book. That language is purposely repeated to emphasize the various ways that our own conduct affects others, whether in a positive or a negative manner. As you will discover, your behavior can make someone's day or damage it, and it's up to you to decide how you "pay it forward." Ultimately, we must bear responsibility for that behavior and its consequences.

The first and last Polite Planet Actions, "Know Who You Are" and "Plant a Seed," are somewhat more internally focused; the fifty in between these two bookends are based more on interactive behavior with others. The range of included topics is not exhaustive, nor is each chapter encyclopedic. Rather, the actions are guidelines to stimulate your own thinking and springboards that spur further exploration. As you read through these suggested actions, keep in mind the large and small ways that your treatment of people can and does make a difference. The most enriching and satisfying revelation may well be the one that you find within yourself, as you connect more deeply with others and more fully realize and embrace our shared humanity. Toward that end, let us all take steps together toward creating a more civilized society and a polite planet.

The Polite Planet Action Guide

How You Can Be Part of the Solution

Know Who You Are

He who knows others is wise.
He who knows himself is enlightened.
—LAO TZU

Behavior is the mirror in which everyone shows
their image.
—JOHANN WOLFGANG VON GOETHE

Human beings are intelligent but also cunning, especially as we use our wits to spot the faults of others, but justify, ignore, or simply refuse to see our own. Knowing who we are and how we relate to others is a lifelong journey, particularly as we age. A thirteen-year-old thinks, relates to, and behaves in the world differently from someone who is thirty-five, fifty, or seventy. Misbehavior attributed to youth might not be so easily excused when we become adults. By that point, we are expected to have learned appropriate and respectful conduct, and attained an ability to curb destructive impulses. But does that always happen?

We get busy, caught up in our own rushed and stressed lives; in the process, we often become desensitized to and detached from those around us. We see that a lot of other people aren't behaving very nicely or treating others kindly, which doesn't provide much incentive for us to act any differently. Bad manners and incivility, after all, are not against the law. Unfortunately, given that social disapproval isn't what it used to be, the only finger shaming us is our own. However, awareness of your own conduct, coupled with a commitment to change, can be life altering, becoming a magical needle, mending the deteriorating fabric of society.

What is inside us ultimately shows on the outside. Our thoughts, emotions, personality and character traits, beliefs, values, and attitudes all influence our outward behavior and the way we treat others—respectfully and with consideration, or not. For example, a haughty or snobbish person may display that attitude physically, with "her nose stuck up in the air." Someone who has "a chip on his shoulder" can reflect that outlook in his body language. Of course, there are other ways that we inadvertently express negative attitudes—disdainful, mocking, or sneering facial expressions; hurtful words; and a condescending tone of voice are but a few examples. The same is true, however, for positive attitudes; I can't imagine empathy, compassion, or joy being expressed with a stone-face.

> Everyone thinks of changing the world, but no one thinks of changing himself.
>
> —LEO TOLSTOY

We each must be aware of our strengths and limitations and be responsible for our actions rather than blaming others. Everyone has negative emotions—anger, hostility, contempt, resentment, fear, and even hate—which, at times, serve a useful purpose.

When those emotions are not managed or expressed appropriately, however, they become destructive and harmful to others, as well as to ourselves, which is why self-restraint is such an important element of our conduct. It's not merely what we *do*, but it's often what we *don't do* that matters. Insight into how we typically react in given situations can help us curb our negative responses, diminishing later regret.

> The opposite of love is not hate; it's indifference.
>
> —ELIE WIESEL

Sometimes we are oblivious or unconscious of the effect of our actions, or are inured to other people's feelings, which impacts and damages our relationships. If our disconnection from people and our community is, in part, a result of our negative behaviors, why not change our conduct for the better?

We must *become consciously aware of our behavior and how we treat others*, focusing daily on the positive intentions behind our actions, so that we can constructively connect and interact with the people in our lives, whether we know them well or not. We also must take the time to *see, hear,* and *pay attention* to the people in our midst.

This book is about making connections with people, and how to develop and maintain them in a fast-paced, ever-changing world. The greater objective is how we, as individuals, can do our part to shape a more civilized society and a politer planet. As you read through the following chapters, take the time to reflect on your own behavior. Consider how your respectful and considerate actions might influence people around you. Then imagine all those positive ripples emanating as a result of what you do and how you behave. Going forward, you may even want to develop a personal inventory sheet, an honest behavioral assessment. Note whether you exude genuine respect and consideration for others, or at times, behave like a jerk. Do you truly listen to another point of view, or do you endlessly rationalize your own? Are you generous, empathetic, and compassionate, or more concerned with getting your share? Are you nice or nasty? Passive-aggressive or direct in your communication? Do you manipulate others to get what you want, or are you straightforward in your actions? Further, do you believe that we all bear responsibility for our shared humanity?

> Change will never happen when people lack the ability and courage to see themselves for who they are.
>
> —BRYANT H. McGILL

None of us is perfect. However, to excuse all our imperfections with the line "I'm only human" is a cop-out. Each of us can do better. What it takes is desire and commitment.

Live in the Present Moment

> The secret of health for both mind and body is not
> to mourn for the past, worry about the future,
> or anticipate troubles, but to live in the
> present moment wisely and earnestly.
>
> —BUDDHA

Before we can connect with others, we have to be able to connect with ourselves, and we can only accomplish that by living fully in the present, not the past or the future. When we live in the past, we are often hanging on to anger, resentment, or sadness that colors our current outlook. The Buddhist parable below sheds some wisdom:

> Two monks were traveling together down a muddy road. Along the way they encountered a lovely young woman dressed in a silk kimono and sash, unable to cross the road without soiling her garments. The first monk obligingly lifted her up, carried her across the mud, and then continued on his journey. Unable to speak for hours, but no longer able to restrain himself, the second monk finally asked the first, "Why did you pick up that young woman when you know that we are forbidden to touch females?" The first monk replied, "I left the girl back there hours ago, but you are still carrying her."

Likewise, when we spend our time living in the future, we may be anxious and fearful about what may never happen at all. Or we're so busy with overscheduled agendas that we allow the clock to rule our lives, causing us to miss out on what is happening here and now. Either way, we shortchange ourselves, and those in our circle, because we are too busy to stop, smell the roses, and connect with one another. Promises to "get together" go unfulfilled. When we do actually meet, we're frequently so preoccupied that we're not present at all, causing us to miss out on the richness of the moment. We do this with our families as well as our friends. Our kids grow up and are gone, and what we remember are the days when we frantically shuttled them to a myriad of activities, when we should have had a few more picnics.

It's a fact that our lives are hectic, making it difficult, at times, to catch our breath, much less relax, but that's exactly what we have to do in order to stay grounded and centered. While the following tactics may sound clichéd to some or silly to those who have never tried them, a substantial body of scientific study has proven their benefits. Try incorporating them into your daily regimen. The stillness of those serene moments, when you cease racing and are fully present, can provide wisdom and insight, as well as rejuvenation for the mind, body, and spirit.

At least once a day, stop, close your eyes, and breathe deeply, clearing your mind of any clutter. Concentrate on nothing else but each breath as it flows in and out of your body for as long as you can manage. Practicing this for even five minutes can do wonders!

Take time to notice and absorb the beauty of nature around you. Get lost in the magnificence of a tree or the perfection of a flower; notice the warmth of the sun's rays on your cheeks, the feeling of your feet on the ground as you walk, or the sound of a breeze rustling leaves.

Exercise as often as possible, working out tensions through physical activity while making your body healthier and stronger. Try other stress-relieving techniques such as yoga or meditation. A friend of mine who teaches yoga is so practiced that she is able to drop into her body during the few minutes she is in a grocery store line, achieving deep relaxation.

> One of the most tragic things I know about human nature is that all of us tend to put off living. We are all dreaming of some magical rose garden over the horizon— instead of enjoying the roses that are blooming outside our windows today.
>
> —DALE CARNEGIE

If you have memories from the past, concentrate on the joy of the good ones rather than brooding about those that bring you pain. I'm not suggesting, for instance, that you never feel sad, particularly over the memories of lost loved ones. However, allow yourself to fully feel that sadness *in the moment*, so that you work through it, and are able to feel joy again.

If you want to be close to and connect with others, be *with them*, here and now, not lost in your thoughts, judgments, or agenda. While we have memories of the past, the present moment is what is real, because the future hasn't yet happened.

Smile

The shortest distance between
two people is a smile.
—ANONYMOUS

For people who want to positively impact the world around them but have no idea how, I have a simple suggestion ... just *smile*. This gesture, which is so seemingly small and effortless, can have far-reaching consequences, for the more you smile, the more positive reactions you elicit, both within yourself and within others. These good feelings are contagious and generate a ripple effect as they pass from one person to another in an ever-widening pool. Smiling facilitates *connection*.

Walking down a street, for instance, you look at a complete stranger who smiles at you. And what do you do in return? Smile. Daniel Goleman, author of *Social Intelligence*, attributes this near-automatic reflex to mirror neurons that detect the smiles of others and trigger our own—in a sense, bridging us brain to brain. He refers to the work of Swedish researchers who found that simply looking at a picture of a happy face can cause the muscles around our mouths to momentarily pull upward into a smile. This activity can have biological effects as well: Our facial expressions will actually evoke the same feelings within us.

Goleman writes, "Smiles have an edge over all other emotional expressions: the human brain prefers happy faces, recognizing them more readily and quickly than those with negative expressions—an effect known as the 'happy face advantage.'" Further, he cites the findings of some neuroscientists who claim that the brain is primed toward positive feelings, generating more upbeat moods than negative ones, resulting in a more positive outlook on life. Goleman suggests that nature tends to foster positive relationships;

while human aggression cannot be negated, "we are not innately primed to dislike people from the start."

So what does the smile mean? Besides being a key symbol of human happiness, Dr. Dacher Keltner, author of *Born to Be Good*, writes, "In evolution's toolbox of adaptations that promote cooperation, the smile is perhaps the most potent tool." It is visible from afar, triggers activation in the reward centers of the brain, and is beneficial to both the smiler and the recipient. A smile can bring out the best in each of us, making it a major contributor to our social integration.

The first known researcher to study the smile scientifically was French neurologist Guillaume Duchenne de Boulogne who, in the nineteenth century, conducted experiments by electrically stimulating facial muscles and analyzing the resulting expressions. He determined that two groups of muscles controlled the smiling reflex, but only one of them produced a genuine "enjoyment" smile.

The zygomatic major muscles that run down the side of the face connect with and pull back the corners of the mouth, exposing the teeth and enlarging the cheeks. Since these muscles are consciously controlled, they enable us to generate a "fake smile"—one that is not induced by pure happiness, pleasure, or enjoyment. This type of smile developed through evolution so that humans could appear submissive and, thus, friendly to oncoming strangers.

The orbicularis oculis muscle group, on the other hand, involuntarily controls the muscles around the eyes, causing them to narrow with crow's feet at their edges when someone is genuinely happy. Because this muscle group is very difficult to control voluntarily, Duchenne determined that this smile cannot be created at will, or under false conditions; therefore, it is considered the only "genuine" smile and commonly referred to today as the "Duchenne smile."

Dr. Paul Ekman, an eminent psychologist from the University of California, built on Duchenne's findings, incorporating them into his own research on communicating emotion through facial expressions and body language, which he began in 1954 and continues today. As part of his Facial Action Coding System (FACS), developed in conjunction with his partner, Dr. Wallace V. Friesen of the University of Kentucky, he determined that there were eighteen different smiles, involving various combinations of fifteen facial muscles. Among them are a pained grin-and-bear-it smile, a cruel smile, a liar's smile, a tight-lipped "I've got a secret" smile, a fearful smile, a smile of relief, and a submissive "I'm here to serve you" smile. However, only the Duchenne smile, which Ekman later referred to as the D smile, carries with it feelings of positive emotion.

In *Born to Be Good*, Keltner presents findings that support the many positive ways that D smiles affect our lives, such as forging the bonding between mother and child, and diminishing our levels of stress. Further, perceiving the smiles of others triggers the release of the neurotransmitter dopamine, which promotes friendliness and affiliation, and facilitates trust and social well-being.

In the landmark Mills Longitudinal Study, Dr. Ravenna Helson, of the University of California, Berkeley, began following 110 graduates of Mills College, from the classes of 1959 and 1960, studying their adult development up to the present day. The women, who are now over seventy years old, are participants in what has been the longest longitudinal study of the lives of women ever conducted. In 1999, as part of the investigation, researchers examined the women's graduation photos, comparing the development of the lives of those whose pictures displayed D smiles against those who did not. Dr. Keltner, who worked with the photos, reported that the women with the warmer D smiles when they were twenty "reported less anxiety, fear, sadness, pain, and despair on a daily basis for the next thirty years.... They also reported feeling more connected to those around them."

> Peace begins with a smile.
> —MOTHER TERESA

The D smile graduates, as a result of their sense that they were achieving their goals, "became more organized, mentally focused, and achievement oriented." When the women were brought to the UC Berkeley campus, the women with the warmer smiles made more favorable impressions on the scientists working with them as well as on other individuals. They were also determined to have more fulfilling marriages.

While studies proving the positive effects of smiling are enlightening, it is worthwhile to consider how smiling plays out in your own life and how it makes you feel. As for myself, when I greet my family (or they greet me) in the morning with a cheerful smile, the day just starts out better. Walking down the street or a corridor, I enjoy having people smile at me and vice versa. And even though it may not be a D smile, when the news is bad, it is comforting to talk with a loving person whose compassionate smile says, "I care about you."

Smile genuinely and often. According to researcher and behavioral change expert Dr. Mark Stibich, smiling—particularly the Duchenne smile—has many benefits: It boosts the immune system, reduces stress, lowers blood pressure, and positively affects people's perceptions of you. Many career coaches advise their clients to smile when talking on the phone because their voices can actually sound more positive and friendlier. Allan and Barbara Pease, authors of *The Definitive Book of Body Language*, report that "research in courtrooms shows that an apology offered with a smile incurs a lesser penalty than an apology without one." The same authors also affirm that smiling at appropriate times during a sales and negotiating process results in more successful outcomes.

At its best, a joyful smile reflects happiness. In another context, it serves as an act of kindness and empathy. Smiling can bridge the gap between two people, promoting cooperation and collaboration. Smiling, without a doubt, is the great connector.

$$\sim\!\!\!\sim 4 \sim\!\!\!\sim$$

See Yourself as Others See You

Sometimes you can't see yourself clearly until you
see yourself through the eyes of others.
—ELLEN DEGENERES

The face is the mirror of the mind, and eyes
without speaking confess the secrets of the heart.
—ST. JEROME

When we look at our image in the mirror, how many of us take just
a cursory glance—quickly straightening a tie, combing a loose hair
into place, removing a smudge of lipstick—without taking stock of our
countenance and how we really appear?

Few of us realize what is at stake with our own appearance, for what we
think and feel on the inside is likely to show externally to the outside
world, for better or for worse. Through facial expressions and body language, we are apt to "wear" our thoughts, convictions, emotions, and attitudes. We inevitably radiate positive or negative "vibes" that are visible and
sometimes palpable to those around us.

The way we appear plays a large part in how others perceive and react
to us, and can literally bring them closer to us or push them away.
Obviously, if your face bears a warm and friendly expression, you're much
more likely to attract and connect with people than if you exude a menac-
ing and antagonizing demeanor. Body language that conveys confidence
and interest in other people is more inviting than a stance with arms folded

across the chest, indicating a lack of approachability or possibly judgment. Thus, it is beneficial for each of us to develop a more focused awareness of our own image and to take an extra moment to check in a mirror how we *really* look before we venture out into public.

If asked to name our primary form of communication, most people would say speech. However, most experts agree that words are used mainly to convey information, and that our interpersonal attitudes and feelings are communicated largely through body language and facial expressions. Consider, for example, how a mother's reproachful gaze speaks volumes to her misbehaving child without uttering a word.

Our human verbal language began to develop somewhere between 500,000 and two million years ago; before that, all communication was nonverbal. Safety and survival often depended on our forebears' ability to accurately read the facial expressions and body language of a fellow primate, assessing him as friend or foe. As Daniel Goleman explains in *Social Intelligence*, we do much the same today, guided by the involuntary impulses fielded by our hypervigilant amygdala, an almond-shaped area deep within the midbrain that triggers a response of fight, flight, or freeze. Our ability to communicate nonverbally, however, extends beyond the scope of determining danger.

Initially, Charles Darwin explored the concept of facial expressions, publishing *The Expression of Emotions in Man and Animals* in 1876. Beginning in the 1950s, Dr. Albert Mehrabian, professor emeritus of psychology at UCLA, furthered this study with landmark research on body language and facial expressions. Mehrabian concluded that, in face-to-face communication, feelings and attitudes are conveyed by three factors: facial expression and body language, voice tone and inflection, and words. When there is a lack of congruity between the verbal and nonverbal expressions, Mehrabian reported that the nonverbal messages carry greater sway.

For instance, if I say to you, "That is the most beautiful dress I have ever seen," but I simultaneously shake my head no, that is a mixed message, giving rise to doubt and confusion, because my facial expression and body language conflict with the words. A listener will more likely trust the nonverbal communication while disbelieving the words. According to Mehrabian, to determine which message is correct, the brain will come to a conclusion based 55 percent on how a person looks, 38 percent on how she sounds, and 7 percent on her actual words. The impact of the nonverbal factors, thus, amounts to 93 percent of what you perceive.

What all this means is that, face-to-face, your nonverbal messages play as vital a role as the verbal ones do. For example, if you are verbally apologizing to a person but do so with a condescending tone of voice or a smirk on your face, your apology will probably not be accepted as genuine. Or, if you are trying to hide something, your deception may become evident through your anxious mannerisms.

My Social IQ seminars stress the importance of first impressions, particularly in job interviews. Your interest and enthusiasm won't come across if your face shows no animation and you slump while standing or sitting. Your professionalism and confidence will shine through based on how well you speak, the ease and comfort you project, the firmness of your handshake, and your appropriate attire. If you're perspiring profusely, fidgeting with your hands, and looking up at the ceiling when answering a question, you'll hardly project equanimity.

Silent, nonverbal messages are also displayed with your eyes, for in Western cultures, connecting through eye contact is vital. If you continually cast your eyes downward toward the floor, you may send a message that you're bored, apathetic, or shy. Eyes that nervously dart around the room may give the impression of shiftiness, making you appear untrustworthy. On the other hand, being able to comfortably look into another person's eyes may demonstrate a high level of confidence, interest, and professionalism.

The point of all this is to be aware of your own image and how you may be coming across to other people. Your facial expressions and body language communicate the feelings and attitudes that you have about yourself as well as what you think of others. They play a crucial role in the way you connect with people around you and the quality of your interpersonal relationships.

Above all, it is important to understand that, whatever you do, it is virtually impossible *not* to communicate. If you stand in a room and say or do nothing, you will send a message that will be perceived by others, regardless of whether or not those perceptions are based in reality. As for your own reality, take a long and serious gaze in the mirror; that is an important start to developing self-awareness and the ability to see yourself as others see you. Afterward, go out there and "put your best foot forward"!

How's that for body language?

5

Sharpen Your Social Antenna

The most important thing in communication is
to hear what isn't being said.
—PETER F. DRUCKER

I think the one lesson I have learned is that
there is no substitute for paying attention.
—DIANE SAWYER

My Social IQ seminars focus on enriching our social aptitude and communication skills in order to deepen our interpersonal relationships and positively connect with people. The point is not only to address how we present ourselves and come across to others, but also to develop a heightened sense of awareness of and sensitivity to the people with whom we are interacting. I encourage students to elevate their *social antenna*, which, like radar, picks up on the social cues of others, detecting and correctly perceiving their moods, feelings, and attitudes.

Communication is a two-way process between people. However, there are things *you* can do to become a better communicator: Show genuine interest in others by asking questions and actively listening, and develop your social antenna by observing their social cues—verbal as well as nonverbal.

The face has almost two hundred muscles, most of which are around the eyes, referred to by some as the "windows to the soul"; as such, the eyes can often reveal what is going on inside a person. When talking face-to-face with someone, take an opportunity to consciously notice the nuances of the person's expressions, which not only can help you gain insight into what a person may be thinking or feeling but also can give you a cue as to what you should say or how to react. For example, if you see that someone momentarily flinches or is taken aback by something you have just said, clarify whether what you said is disturbing or disagreeable. If your conversation partner does not laugh at your joke, be attuned to her reaction: Either she might not understand your humor or she might have been offended by it. Note whether a smile seems to be genuine or is more of a pained or perfunctory expression.

The most renowned expert in interpreting the emotional content of facial expressions is Dr. Paul Ekman of the University of California, whose research over the past forty years continues today. In his early work, he became known for his identification of expressions of human emotion, which he deemed to be *universal* among humankind. Up to that point, anthropologists like Margaret Mead had considered such expressions to be culturally determined. Ekman, however, found that anger, disgust, fear, joy, sadness, and surprise are manifested in facial expressions shared by people in virtually all cultures. Later, he developed the aforementioned FACS—the Facial Action Coding System—in which he recorded the permutations of virtually every conceivable facial expression. In time, his research expanded to other areas, incorporating a fuller complement of body language. Much of his study has concentrated on nonverbal signs of lying; Ekman's expertise enables him to pick up on facial clues that point to a defendant's deception or guile.

Interestingly, women are generally much better observers and interpreters of body language and facial expressions than men are. Just by watching what is going on between two people, women are far better than men at picking up on the emotional content in relationships—who is getting along with whom, if there is tension between a couple, and so forth. Magnetic resonance imaging (MRI) results show that women have fourteen to sixteen receptors in their brains to assess such behavioral information as opposed to four to six in the male brain. (Women also are endowed with a greater range of peripheral vision, up to forty-five degrees, allowing them to maintain eye contact while taking in a wider scope than men can manage. As an offset, perhaps, men have more acute long-distance vision than do their feminine counterparts, although their close-up range falls far below the capability of women.)

Fortunately or not, we cannot totally fake body language for a long period, masking our feelings, attitudes, falsehoods, or guilt. While some gestures, such as open palms (indicating truthful sincerity), can be learned and employed, there are other microsignals—such as pupil dilation, sweating, and blushing—that will "leak" our true feelings and inevitably expose any pretense. That said, however, we can develop positive body language such as an erect posture.

The Definitive Book of Body Language by Allan and Barbara Pease is a treasure trove of tips on body language and techniques that help foster connections with people. According to the authors:

- Look at "clusters" of body language signs, rather than focusing on a singular one. That is the best way to read a person.

- When appropriate, use a "mirroring technique," whereby your facial expressions mimic those of the person with whom you are speaking. Salespeople often use this tactic as a compliment to a client. It is also a safe way to communicate with people of foreign cultures, since you are less likely to offend other people by mirroring their gestures and expressions.

- When talking to a person, notice whether he is more inclined to *lean in* toward the conversation (a reflection of engagement and interest) or *pull back or away* (indicating a desire to disengage). If he pulls away, don't prolong the conversation; the other person may have an agenda that has nothing to do with you.

So by tuning in to the social cues of others, we can establish better connections and build better relationships. While it's possible to misread or misinterpret those messages, it is worse to ignore them or fail to notice them at all. Although we may not choose to spend forty years becoming experts, like Dr. Ekman, we can heighten our awareness of others' physical nuances so that we spot the nonverbal clues, rather than being clueless.

Respect the
Boundaries of Others

And this is one of the major questions of our lives:
how we keep boundaries, what permission we have
to cross boundaries, and how we do so.

—A. B. YEHOSHUA

No doubt, you've had one of these experiences: Someone behind you in line stands a little too close to your body; a stranger takes the seat right next to you in a movie theater when most other seats are vacant; or the person to whom you were just introduced is so "in your face" he could almost bite your nose off. In each of these situations, an "intruder" has broken an unspoken rule—violating your invisible personal space—moving within your territorial "bubble," which is a little too close for your comfort.

The term for this, *proxemics*, was coined by anthropologist Edward T. Hall in the 1960s. His studies determined that there is a set of measurable space between people as they interact with one another, depending on the situation. Hall established these nonverbal spaces, which he categorized as follows:

- *Intimate* distance—from zero to eighteen inches—for whispering, touching, or hugging. Strangers in this close proximity, on a subway, for instance, will feel discomfort; as the senses become overwhelmed, people become agitated and seek to withdraw.

- *Personal* distance—from eighteen inches to four feet—among family or good friends. Hall maintained that while this space creates a reasonable amount of distance, it is still close enough for most people to touch one another.

- *Social* distance—from four to twelve feet—interactions among acquaintances. This is the most common interpersonal distance among businesspeople and more formal social relationships.

- *Public* distance—from twelve feet on—for public speaking. Hall also maintained that this distance is sufficient space for self-defense.

When these distances are not observed, people will have varied reactions, depending on the situation. In order to avoid intimacy, they may begin to divert their eyes, reveal disgust or irritation on their faces, glare at the person, inch away, or demonstrate other body language that shows discomfort, such as stiffening up. Our blood pressure may rise, our heart rate may increase, and our palms may sweat, says David B. Givens, director of the Center for Nonverbal Studies in Spokane, Washington. In his studies, Hall also determined that these are standards that apply to most Americans, but not necessarily to people in other cultures. People in Latin countries, for instance, generally maintain much closer contact than people in the United States, and they are more inclined to touch one another. Middle Easterners, it has been observed, can stand so close that they will almost be nose-to-nose in conversations. Nordic people and those from the Netherlands, on the other hand, generally keep greater distances. Some Asians maintain a greater distance than North Americans do, keeping in mind that it takes at least three feet between people in order to bow so as not to knock heads. In general, most Asian businesspeople keep a certain distance in other ways, because they are more formal than Americans, employing proper surnames rather than referring to one another on a first-name basis. As a result, in cross-cultural interactions, Americans are often perceived as being too familiar and informal. The implications for developing interpersonal relationships and connections in global business are apparent as people in one culture begin to understand one another and make allowances and adjustments—or not—based on personal preferences.

Besides studying spaces between people, proxemic researchers also assist urban planners, developers, and industry executives in understanding how we travel through public spaces, how we shop, and which sorts of spaces we find most comfortable. They also research the layout and design of our homes. Say Terri Morrison and Wayne A. Conway, authors of *Kiss, Bow, or Shake Hands*, North American families live "more alone" than any other people in the world, for whom living with extended families is more common. American homes generally have more rooms, often with each child having his own. Shortly after larger American-style homes began to be built in Japan, family members, who had previously spent most of their time together in the same room, retreated to separate rooms; this was blamed, say the authors, for all sorts of social ills. The same trend, they say, is beginning to develop in China, where larger houses are beginning to be built for the growing middle class.

Space is defined not just as personal space, but also as what we have been assigned. A desk, for instance, in a corporate environment is considered *ours*. We would consider it quite rude if someone were to go through our desk drawers, even if she were looking for one of *our* pens or paper clips. Our sense of space in that environment also extends to our office cubicles, where we are separated from our coworkers by divider panels extending from the floor to just over our heads. The same sense of possession can apply at home.

Apparently we love our own cell phones but we hate everyone else's.

—JOE BOB BRIGGS

Boundary lines exist in public spaces that we all share, too. We each have a right to enjoy these public spaces, as long as we don't infringe on other people's enjoyment. Cell-phone abuse is a pervasive complaint. However, it's not just cell phones; it can be any conversation—in a movie theater, in a restaurant, on an airplane—in which a person's voice is so loud that no one else can think, hear, or talk. These disruptions impede our own pleasure in arenas that we've also paid to enjoy. We see this kind of lack of consideration in over-rowdiness at a sporting event, playing music that annoys the neighbors, or having a wild late-night party in a hotel room when other guests are sleeping down the hall. In any of these situations, our intrusions infringe on the rights and enjoyment of others who have the same right to be there as we do, so that we take more than our share, more than we are entitled to.

Shared spaces also require that we don't take up too much room, as in hogging a sidewalk, standing two abreast on an escalator so that others cannot pass, grabbing both armrests for yourself on an airplane or in a movie theatre, or crowding an overhead airline bin with all our stuff. The air that we breathe is also shared, which necessitates another form of consideration for others: The secondhand smoke generated from cigarettes, cigars, or pipes is more than annoying—it can kill you! Along the same lines, be discreet in your use of cologne; it can be offensive to others in intimate public spaces such as waiting rooms (where people may be sick) or a classroom.

Another issue that should be mentioned is backing off when someone says no. We should never assume, whether it is taking liberties on a date or accosting someone with an overzealous sales pitch, that *No* means *Maybe* or *Ask me again* or *Tell me more. No* should suffice as a firm and complete answer, as a means of establishing boundaries. It is also a useful response when we have overcommitted to too many projects!

> Boundaries are to protect life, not to limit pleasures.
>
> —EDWIN LOUIS COLE

In a world that is increasingly dense, with a growing population, our respect for boundaries and space is essential. Whether it is keeping our hands off of other people's belongings—as well as their bodies—or sharing the same space with consideration for everyone's enjoyment, the way in which we live and move about is vital to getting along. It is paying deference to everyone's right to be here, including your own.

7

Listen Up

Most of the successful people I've known are the
ones who do more listening than talking.
—BERNARD M. BARUCH

My mother-in-law, a schoolteacher for thirty years, used to say, "It's impossible to learn anything if your mouth is always open!" While I did not always agree with her, I do concur when it comes to listening.

Although the human brain endows us with a complex array of communication skills, we don't always use them to their fullest extent, particularly when it comes to listening. Not only are we prone to making more errors when not actively listening, but also we are often blatantly rude in the process.

Listening and truly hearing another person begins with *being present*, which means giving an individual your undivided attention. As American psychiatrist and author M. Scott Peck once wrote, "You cannot truly listen to anyone and do anything else at the same time." There's nothing more flattering, in fact, than making a person feel like he's the only person in the world when you're talking to him. As such, listening becomes the great connector.

It is not possible to be fully engaged or concentrate on what someone else is saying if your head is in the clouds, or if you're mentally compiling "to do lists," or multitasking in cyberspace. Listening also enables you to converse with greater facility. If, for example, you are constantly thinking about what you're going to say next, rather than concentrating on the other person's words, you will miss out on important verbal cues that can be vital prompts or segues to your follow-up response—springboards for your next comment. Conversation, thus, flows more naturally, so you can develop better rapport. Better to suffer an awkward pause than to run a mile a minute in your head without listening.

It takes self-awareness to know whether you are actively listening. If, for instance, you find yourself ...

constantly interrupting

zoning out, unable to concentrate

finishing a person's sentences or rushing him along

misinterpreting the context of what someone is saying

focusing on what you want out of that person—such as a job— or thinking about how much money he makes, or where she bought that dress

changing the subject at will and controlling the dialogue

eavesdropping on nearby conversations

gazing beyond a person's shoulder for someone more interesting to meet ...

then you are not in listening mode. If someone looks at you with a horrified expression after you just exclaimed, "How wonderful!" you might want to check whether he just told you that his favorite pet died, as that would definitely be a sign that you were not listening.

Good dialogue should be a two-way street. No one is interested in hearing someone who, enamored of the sound of his own voice, monopolizes a conversation and becomes a boor. Ask questions and show genuine interest in what the other person has to say.

Putting effort and energy into social interactions by being open and curious can make the difference between what scientists describe as "high-maintenance" and "low-maintenance" interactions. Without curiosity stimulating the flow of conversation between two people, it is more difficult to establish a connection with another person, turning the exchange into one that is higher maintenance. Todd Kashdan, George Mason University professor of psychology and author of *Curious?*, points to research that has shown that open and curious people are more likely to recognize the emotions of other people and rapidly synchronize with them as they fluctuate from moment to moment. This process also helps us work together and understand what others are thinking and doing, in a series of low-maintenance interactions. (Curious people, by the way, are often well liked, partly because they have a wide range of interests about which they can talk easily, and also because they share information about themselves.)

Texting, answering a cell phone, or working on a computer while someone else is talking—in person or during a phone call—is not simply impolite; it can hurt someone's feelings. In effect, you are sending a message that can be interpreted as: "My time is more important than yours" or "You don't deserve my undivided attention" or "I'm not interested in what you have to say." If you take a call while talking with someone else, it is the equivalent of turning your back on that person, which, when you think about it, is a pretty shabby way to treat someone. Also bear in mind that, if you multitask during a telephone conversation, the person on the other end may actually *hear* your lack of attention as you click the keyboard of a computer or shuffle papers in the background.

An important benefit of listening is learning, which brings me back to my mother-in-law's comment about the wisdom of judiciously keeping one's mouth closed. Listening gives you time—time to stand back and make assessments, time to get to know people and their points of view, time to gather information to formulate your own opinions. Listening also gives you an opportunity to think and reflect. It often prevents your making snap judgments and jumping to conclusions before obtaining the facts, speaking out of turn, or uttering stupid statements that you may later regret.

Careful listening is critical in many professions. The primary job of a juror is to listen, as well as to observe, in order to evaluate and weigh evidence. A physician must listen to a patient's history, as well as her heart, in order to make a proper medical diagnosis. A salesperson listens to understand a customer's problems and needs. Leaders often reach compromises through negotiation, in which listening plays a vital role.

I only wish I could find an institute that teaches people how to listen. Businesspeople need to listen at least as much as they need to talk. Too many people fail to realize that real communication goes in both directions.

—LEE IACOCCA

If we want to be attuned to our relationships—with people we know or those we might want to get to know—we must listen and pay attention to what is being said, as well as to what is not being said. Listening bolsters the ability to "read between the lines" and pick up on social cues. Listening is important in just about everything that we do; in fact, I can't think of a case where it isn't.

Discern the Right Meaning

I know that you believe you understand what you think I said, but I'm not sure you realize that what you heard is not what I meant.
—ROBERT McCLOSKEY

In ancient Greece, citizens sought the wisdom of the Oracle at Delphi before any major undertaking; the conundrum, unfortunately, was the ambiguity of the response, owing to the absence of punctuation. A soldier inquiring about his destiny in battle had to correctly interpret whether the answer was "Go war, return, not die" or "Go war, return not, die." Big difference. While we no longer decipher an Oracle's message today, we still must be attuned during conversations; active listening and clarification helps us hear and also interpret correctly the intent or meaning of what the words actually mean.

We are all prone to seeing any situation through the prism of our own reality, feelings, thoughts, and judgments, so that we misconstrue what the other party is saying. When talking to our spouse, we often assume that we know what our better half is thinking, or his intent or meaning. What we *hear* may well be a projection of what is on our mind, not what he's saying at all. The lack of clarity can get us riled up and on course to blame the other person for something that isn't even part of the issue at hand. Our judgments lead to accusations, or the blame game, which often reveals stockpiled resentments. Unfortunately, this is a process that occurs with our family, our friends, and our colleagues.

Reactive emotion ignites our conversations like a tinderbox and clouds our ability to listen. In a heated discussion in which attacks or accusations are being hurled, listening and "hearing" are apt to vanish. The moment that you become defensive, protecting your own point of view, you cease listening. In these situations, it helps to take a moment, pull back, and become aware of what is actually taking place.

Difficult Conversations: How to Discuss What Matters Most is a gem of a book in which Douglas Stone, Bruce Patton, and Sheila Heen of the Harvard Negotiation Project analyze what frequently happens during such exchanges, territory that is much too rich and complex to cover here. Any discussion that is uncomfortable for *you* is considered a difficult conversation, whether the strain is a result of the topic, the situation, the person, threats to your identity, or vested interests that you may have. As such, difficult conversations share some of the elements of a negotiation. Nonetheless, because the intent or meaning behind words is invisible, the authors offer strategies to decode what is being said so that two parties can achieve greater clarity and mutual understanding without blame, keeping a difficult exchange from going off track.

One strategy is not to assume or prejudge that we already "know" the motivations or intent of the other person, which can quickly derail a conversation. Assumptions, which actor and author Henry Winkler once called "the termites of relationships," can thwart our ability to hear what is being said. Better to clarify by asking a question before launching an attack: "This is what I am hearing you say; is this what you mean?" Also do not assume that you know the whole story, because there may be details that alter your judgment.

Mutual understanding is neither a given nor automatic; active listening and clarifying through simple questions, however, can help pave the way.

9

Strike a Tone

> We often refuse to accept an idea merely because
> the tone of voice in which it has been expressed
> is unsympathetic to us.
> —FRIEDRICH NIETZSCHE

When we speak, our tone may be louder than our words, communicating our intent, emotions, and attitudes. Our tone may convey warmth and friendliness, as well as compassion and sincerity. It can reveal interest or indifference, arrogance or humility, respect or contempt. The sharpness or softness of tone shows our patience or lack of it. Thus, we can "set the tone," so to speak, during any interpersonal interaction, which can potentially impact the outcome of a discussion. That's why "It's not *what* you say but *how* you say it" is not just an idle saying. Your pet dog may not actually understand English, but he knows when to get out of Dodge based on your emphatic and angry tone.

I have come to learn that it is possible to say almost anything, however disagreeable, if presented in a tone that is devoid of anger, belligerence, sarcasm, criticism, superiority, judgment, impatience, or ugliness. When those elements are absent, it's much easier to conduct a dialogue—however polarized—so that issues can be aired and thoughtful opinions can be exchanged.

What often thwarts civil discourse is an underlying negative tone; when it is tinged with a sense that "my viewpoint is better than yours" or "I'm right and you're wrong," all bets are off. More often than not, an acrimonious verbal exchange ensues, halting the free flow of substantive ideas. As a result, the parties rarely forge a solution or compromise. There ceases to be a fair exchange; the argument is with the *person*, not about the *matter in question*. This is as likely to happen in families or among friends as it is in town meetings or on the floor of the Senate.

Because tone reflects intent and emotion, it communicates how we feel about others, which, in turn, can translate into how we make them feel. When laced with a tone of graciousness and interest, our words can make someone feel warm and welcome. Conversely, the same words, when spoken with an edge of anger or sarcasm, can send someone packing. "What are you *doing here*?" when delivered with joy and surprise has a very different meaning than "What are *you* doing here?" which sends the message that perhaps you ought not to be here at all.

Whether addressing our children or business colleagues, we can deliver criticism constructively, so that the recipients feel encouraged and good about themselves. When we deliver the same criticism with a tone of judgment and derision, we accomplish the opposite. Just as words must always be carefully chosen, so must the tone.

Great care also must be extended when we communicate with words on paper—or in cyberspace—because tone is not so easily determined, leading to misunderstandings and hurt feelings. Without the intonation of a physical human voice, the written word can lack clarity, particularly when done in haste. This is more apt to occur in electronic correspondence, such as e-mail and instant messages, which, too often, is spontaneous, abbreviated, casual, and brief. Worse, some e-mails are mistakenly sent before completion. Messages that are typed with uppercase letters (called flaming) can imply screaming, not emphasis. It's better to emphasize by using boldface type or underscoring.

> People will not always remember what you said but will always remember how you made them feel.
>
> —ANONYMOUS

The following exercise points to the hazards of the written word, when tone and emphasis are subject to misinterpretation:

I didn't say that she stole the money (but if I didn't, then someone else did).

I *didn't* say that she stole the money (but, if questioned, I might say so).

I didn't *say* that she stole the money (even though I may have thought so).

I didn't say that *she* stole the money (but someone else obviously did).

I didn't say that she *stole* the money (but she got it somehow).

I didn't say that she stole the *money* (even though other things were missing).

For obvious reasons, face-to-face contact is considered the "warmest" form of communication, providing the benefits of facial expressions and body language, which add context to the human voice. (Skype, with its video capability, offers similar advantages.) The next-warmest form of communication is the telephone, because the human voice, with all of its intonations, is still part of the interaction. For that matter, any interpersonal exchange involving our real voices, in real time, has the added benefit of immediate response, which can provide feedback and clarity. The coldest form of communication is the written word: The handwritten letter is the least distant of these and an e-mail the most.

So whether you are having a lively discussion or exchanging e-mails, take heed of how you sound and don't allow yourself to fall on your own tone-deaf ears. Remember: Tone can speak louder than words.

10

Recognize the
Power of Words

Whatever words we utter should be
chosen with care, for people will hear them and
be influenced by them for good or evil.
—BUDDHA

Speak clearly, if you speak at all;
carve every word before you let it fall.
—OLIVER WENDELL HOLMES

The last Christmas gift that I received from my maternal grandfather, a high school principal, was a dictionary in which he inscribed, "Nothing increases a person's stature more than the ready command of words. Here are several thousand for you to capture and tame." Although I was only ten years old at the time, I was aware, even then, of how much he, a lifelong educator, valued knowledge and having an extensive vocabulary. However, it was not until years later that I began to have a deeper understanding of what my grandfather may have meant.

While building an impressive vocabulary is important, what matters more is recognizing the *power* of words, and how your *choice* of words can speak volumes about who and what you are, as well as what you think and feel. Few factors project your image, and even your character, more than your choice of words, reflective as they are of your intelligence, level of education, beliefs, sophistication, and sensitivity to others. They communicate your logic and the flow of your ideas—or not. Consider, for example, how great eloquence can move a crowd, whereas bad grammar or the inability to speak in complete sentences can undermine your standing and presence as well as your credibility.

Given that they can build as well as destroy, words have extraordinary power. Once spoken or committed to writing and received by another party, they cannot be fully expunged or reclaimed: The residual effect may not be erased from memory, even when forgiveness has been extended. We are generally conscious of whether we mean to convey good or harm, or something in between. Stopping for a second or two to think about the *intent* of our message, before letting the words fly, might alter their selection.

Public figures often make news as a result of verbal gaffes that have various consequences. Politicians who "misspeak" may be forced to retract their words, defend their actual intent, express remorse, apologize, and in some cases, even resign. In 2002, Senator Trent Lott of Mississippi was highly criticized for his remarks, interpreted as racially insensitive, made at the one hundredth birthday celebration of Senator Strom Thurmond, who in 1948 had run for the U.S. presidency as the candidate for the segregationist States Rights Democratic Party. When the media reported his remarks, Lott apologized to an angry public for his poor choice of words, saying that they were certainly not a reflection of his beliefs. Although he remained in office, he was forced to surrender his leadership position in the Senate.

Commenting privately, early in the 2008 presidential campaign, Senator Henry Reid referred to Barack Obama as a black candidate that our electorate would be willing to embrace because he is a "light-skinned African American with no Negro dialect." Reid was admonished for what to many sounded like racial stereotyping, although his public record indicated otherwise. Syndicated radio personality Don Imus fared less well and was ultimately fired for his denigrating description of the women's basketball players at Rutgers University as "nappy-headed hos." And when British Petroleum CEO Tony Hayward said, "I'd like my life back," roughly six weeks after an explosion of his company's oil rig that killed eleven people, followed by the oil spill in the Gulf of Mexico, which created the worst natural disaster in U.S. history, people had no sympathy for him.

Although we can blame some of our verbal slips on thoughtlessness or unfortunate phrasing, the reality is that many stem from our personal beliefs. According to noted psychologist Dr. Florence Kaslow, recent research indicates that declining empathy is one reason for our often shocking word choice. Further, Dr. Kaslow says, "Language is not innocent. We usually say what we mean."

For instance, consider an exchange that I had with a friend who was a French chef in a Parisian restaurant. When I asked him if any female chefs worked there, he replied that there were none because the kitchen was much too small. When I suggested to him that women were generally smaller in size than men and should, therefore, occupy less room, he was speechless. His underlying meaning, I had to assume, was that women were less competent than men and would only take up space better reserved for men. As Dr. Kaslow might say, my friend did not just make a faux pas but revealed a certain stereotype he held regarding female chefs.

Many offensive words have become a part of our everyday vernacular. While *retarded* is a word that can—politically incorrectly—refer to one who is mentally challenged, it is often used these days as a disparaging descriptor of anything that people find objectionable. Saying that someone's clothes are "so gay" is not necessarily a sexual reference; rather, it is an offensive way of labeling another's outfit as being out of the mainstream. In this case, the use of the term *gay* packs a double punch. Beyond being a denigrating description of the clothes, it reinforces, however unintentionally, a connection between being *gay* and being *wrong*. As a result, the speaker is not only insulting the clothes but also an entire group of people. The word *suck* is now so commonly used that its edge has actually diminished: It refers to anything viewed as mildly disagreeable to intolerably disgusting; context and tone indicate its pejorative intensity.

> Language is very powerful. Language does not just describe reality. Language creates the reality it describes.
>
> —ARCHBISHOP DESMOND TUTU

Admittedly, it's hard to go to a movie or anywhere these days without being inundated with profanity, particularly the "F word." The frequency with which it is used, however, does not make it any less coarse or more appropriate, particularly in public. What you do in the privacy of your home or with close associates is personal. However, in public or in your professional life, swearing is not only vulgar but also a sign of a meager vocabulary. It is explosive language that detracts from your image and power.

Swearing can make you appear less professional, less competent, and less in control. A recent international business etiquette survey, commissioned by the Australian company Servcorp Smart Office, reported using swear words as the most hated business behavior, with 79 percent of respondents finding it offensive. Given the multicultural world in which we live, having a more reserved professional demeanor does not make you prudish; it is prudent!

Words have the power to shape our society and, in our world today, the reins on self-expression have largely been lifted. With cascading vulgarity and the proliferation of foul language intended to create shock and awe, a trend reinforced by the media, there is little left in the way of societal disapproval or pressure telling us what not to say or causing us to be shunned or admonished. Therefore, it is up to us to monitor our language, written and verbal. We must rely on our own moral compass to guide us to do the right thing, and to consider the needs and feelings of others. In addition to examining our hearts and conscience, we must tap our intelligence and critical thinking, judging whether we are being smart or stupid. In shaping our words, we also shape who we are; thus, it behooves us to choose them wisely.

> Words have no wings but they can fly a thousand miles.
>
> —KOREAN PROVERB

Working with students for so many decades, my grandfather was undoubtedly challenged by their slang as well as their escapades. Needless to say, he would not recognize the world as it is today, more than fifty years after his passing. What has not changed, however, is that words still have remarkable power not just to communicate but also to influence. If he were here today, I'd assure him that I'm still working on capturing and taming those 25,000 words he passed on to me long ago. However, I would also tell him how I've learned that words have the power to connect us to or estrange us from others. In that light, I'd like to suggest that you let your words be the mortar that binds, not mortar shells that destroy.

~ 11 ~

Hold Your Tongue

Never miss a chance to keep your mouth shut.
—ROBERT NEWTON PECK

During World War II, soldiers were advised that "loose lips sink ships," lest valuable secrets be divulged to the enemy. It is equally wise counsel today, not in shielding ourselves from an enemy, but in not creating one by saying the wrong thing. Hurtful and insensitive words damage relationships, even if that is not our intent. Therefore, it is often better to bite our tongues than to wag them, which requires forethought and restraint.

At one time or another, we've all inadvertently committed verbal faux pas, blunders in which we "open mouth, insert foot"—myself included. I have stupidly asked a woman when her baby is due, only to discover that she has put on a few extra pounds. In another instance, a friend of mine found himself railing against the folly of the Iraq war, only to discover that he was talking to the father of a soldier stationed there.

In both situations, the blunders were unintentional. Nonetheless, they might have been avoided with greater consideration and sensitivity to topics that, perhaps, should never have been brought up in the first place. If you find that you have dug yourself into a hole, common wisdom suggests that you apologize and stop digging. By thinking ahead, however, these kinds of awkward moments might be avoided altogether.

Conversely, it is difficult to be the person on the other side, at whom an inappropriate or tactless remark has been directed. Do you fire back a stinging rebuke, or do you graciously let the matter slide?

Without pride, I confess that, as a younger adult, I was the queen of zingers, those sharp witticisms intended to make an offender wish that he'd never opened his mouth. With passing years, however, I realize how wrong I was and have since consciously refrained from delivering such quips, because striking back provides only momentary satisfaction, serving no one well in the end. Admittedly, there are times when one of those retorts can be so delicious and sizzling that it almost burns my tongue, but I rely on the lump in my throat to warn me that I'm about to say something that is not very nice.

Avenging punches can also backfire and turn ugly, escalating a thoughtless or stupid remark on one person's part into combative verbal volleyball. Professor P. M. Forni, author of *Choosing Civility*, refers to this sort of exchange as "returning rudeness with rudeness," which, in addition to being impolite and uncivil, showcases the speaker's pettiness and lack of self-control. Biting your tongue, rather than appearing clever at someone else's expense, is usually the more civilized response.

The master of the brilliant rejoinder was Winston Churchill. Although his manners were courtly, his comebacks could pierce an opponent to the core, like a smooth, swift sword. When Lady Nancy Astor once said to him, "Winston, if you were my husband, I'd poison your tea," Churchill shot back, "Nancy, if I were your husband, I'd drink it."

We overlook Churchill's lack of restraint, not just because of his remarkable career and a life well lived, but also because his nimble wit and dazzling repartee were clever and rare, then and now. Nonetheless, adept as he was with turning a phrase, Churchill returned rudeness with rudeness, and with unbridled one-upmanship. (Historians have revealed that Churchill was actually quite impatient, petulant, and peevish, with a temper that frequently flared at those around him.)

What are some other guidelines about what *not* to say? For starters, certain topics are simply taboo, particularly with people whom you don't know well. The infamous three, of course, are religion, sex, and politics, because it is easy to offend a person whose practices and preferences you may not know or may be different from your own. Opinions and convictions regarding these matters are often deeply held with widely divergent and polarized points of view. Discussions, as a result, can become highly charged, heating up very quickly, so it is safer to simply avoid these subjects altogether. Besides, getting into a volatile conversation right off the bat might prevent you from getting to know a person with whom you might otherwise have a great deal in common.

It should be noted, however, that when you know someone well, these topics may be broached, albeit with sensitivity. In fact, as a society, we must learn to deal with divisive issues by openly discussing them respectfully and intelligently. (According to a recent study by the Center for Political Participation at Allegheny College, Americans overwhelmingly believe that civility is not only important to democracy but also possible to achieve, even when disagreement is present.)

While there might be differing perspectives as to whether or not a topic is taboo, most would agree that it is sound advice to refrain from ethnic jokes and off-color humor. You may have no idea of a person's heritage or background and, thus, run a great risk of offending. Many people also have a very low tolerance for anything racy, lewd, or ribald, so beware of some of those punch lines, because humor can be very dicey and provocative. Name-calling is anathema, as are racial slurs, labels, and stereotyping. And when it comes to malicious gossip or spreading rumors, just button down the hatch. Further, it is always wise to speak with kindness, remembering the wisdom of Thumper's daddy: "If you can't say something nice, don't say nothing at all."

> Politeness is the art of choosing among one's real thoughts.
>
> —ABEL STEVENS

Parents should always bear in mind that they should not say anything around their children that they would not like their offspring to repeat publicly. Very young children have not yet developed an awareness of appropriate conversational topics or what may be considered a "good" versus "bad" word, including swearing. If children hear their parents using those words at home, they are likely to curse as well. Parents can make a list of words that they do not want their children to say, and make a concerted effort not to use them in front of their kids. The same goes for any sensitive topic that should remain "family business," or remarks that are the sole domain of adults.

In choosing topics, some common sense has to prevail, as well as sensitivity to people and their particular circumstances. For example, you would never ask a woman, newly widowed, if she plans to marry again. Nor would you tell a stranger that he'd look younger if he lost twenty pounds or wore a toupee! Some subjects are too touchy, no matter how well you know a person. For instance, giving advice, solicited or not, regarding other people's love affairs, children, finances, and personal image is always dangerous territory. So is responding to a loaded-gun question. Husbands know that they are treading in a minefield anytime their wives ask them, "Does this make me look fat?" The smart ones, however, eventually learn that "absolutely not!" is the best answer. You get the picture.

Some questions are too personal to ask or to answer. Unless providing your medical history to a physician, you are not obliged to answer such questions. For instance, if asked the cost of your vacation, you could easily respond, "I don't have a tally, but it was money well spent."

Brutal honesty is often couched with "Don't take this personally, but ..." or "No offense to you, but ..." or "I hate to tell you this, but ..." The problem is that the initial disclaimer does not necessarily soften the words that follow, because they often tend to be painfully personal as well as offensive. It is equally off-putting when the negative intention underlying words makes them piercingly sharp and hurtful. For example, to say to a two-hundred-fifty-pound woman, "My dear, that dress is so becoming to your shape," is not a compliment. Nor are congratulations sincere when they are expressed as, "How wonderful that your son finally got into college!"

This is a topic on which an entire book easily could be written, because there are thousands of situations not included here. Growing up, surrounded with numerous family members who neither minced nor measured their words, I learned much about what not to say. Once, my maternal grandmother, upon seeing her newborn grandson, said to her daughter-in-law, "Why, Virginia, that's the ugliest baby I've ever seen; he looks just like you!" So while there is much more that could be said about what not to say, my grandmother's remark pretty much says it all.

❧ 12 ❧

Resist Rhetoric

Education is the most powerful weapon which
you can use to change the world.
—NELSON MANDELA

The recipe for perpetual ignorance is:
Be satisfied with your opinions and
content with your knowledge.
—ELBERT HUBBARD

We are living in the midst of the Information Age, or the Digital Age, in which we have instant access to more information than humanity has ever had before. It is ironic, however, that given all the knowledge available to us at a keystroke, we sometimes fail to seize opportunities for learning. A recent Harvard Business School newsletter reported that less than half of American adults read a book after leaving school, while only 15 to 25 percent read books on a regular basis. Thanks to the Internet, news travels around the world faster than a speeding bullet; delivered in miniparagraphs, however, it often lacks the depth and perspective offered by experienced reporters. Interest in serious journalism, which provides more in-depth coverage, is waning; major newspapers are closing, as news bureaus worldwide shrink.

To capture our attention, broadcast news is encapsulated in brief sound bites. We garner information from the newsmakers who may have spun stories to their best advantage. When rabid rhetoric is in full swing, ideologues pontificate those sound bites, often taken out of context, for the purpose of intentional distortion. Objectivity vanishes.

Events that occur at breakneck speed reveal how interconnected our world is. Almost daily we are reminded of the ramifications of that interconnection: If a pin drops in a small country on one continent, we feel its prick on our skin all around the globe. For example, in the spring of 2010, when Hungary was facing a potential debt crisis, world financial markets entered a downward spiral. Although Hungary's economy is small, her potential default on loans would have had a devastating effect on banks around the world that had lent the country money. If there were ever a time when we need to be alert and informed, it is now. It's necessary to dig below the surface to obtain and weigh our information, but we also need to be particular about where we gather it. To make informed judgments, we must seek knowledge, think, and discern what is fact and what is not.

> Being ignorant is not so much a shame, as being unwilling to learn.
>
> —BEN FRANKLIN

Why can spin be harmful? A story that has been formulated by a "spin doctor" will have been manipulated in order to present its protagonist in the best light. Facts can be selectively chosen with others eliminated altogether in order to provide a positive twist on the story (lies by omission); denials can be reframed ("I didn't know"); euphemisms may be employed; attention may be deflected toward another issue. The "selling points" of the story or newsmaker are spotlighted, rather than the underlying facts that point toward truth. We expect that sort of crafted message when we're buying cars or cosmetics; our news, however, should not be a public relations campaign. Determining what is truth and what is fiction requires diligence. With the Internet in play, Winston Churchill's quotation, "A lie gets halfway around the world before the truth has a chance to get its pants on" has even greater relevance and resonance today than it did decades ago.

Truth itself is a sticky wicket because it is not always absolute. In the words of Nobel Prize winner André Gide, "The color of truth is gray." Our beliefs, knowledge, and experiences shape and impact what is *our truth*; that is, what is true for me may not be the same for you. However, the truth is seldom found in the extremes but somewhere in the middle of any issue. As the late renowned journalist Walter Cronkite wisely noted, "In seeking truth you have to get both sides of a story." In a time of polarized politics, underscored by divergent ideologies, it pays to be curious and ask questions. We must each take the time to examine issues carefully with a fact-based focus. There is a danger in swallowing whole the inflammatory statements of demagogues who demonize the other side and promulgate a single truth. It is imperative for us to recognize red-hot rhetoric for what it is—language intended to play upon and incite the emotion of a crowd, resulting in a mob mentality no longer capable of thinking clearly. Solutions require careful consideration of all opinions, intelligently viewed from all sides, and presented without intentional distortion and without shredding the truth.

It is our responsibility to educate ourselves, seeking knowledge with an open mind and thinking intelligently. This task is just as important in our home lives—as parents, spouses, and children—as it is in public life when it comes to local and global issues. Rabid rhetoric sizzles, but it never promotes the quest for truth or solutions.

Disagree Agreeably

Whenever you're in conflict with someone,
there is one factor that can make the difference
between damaging your relationship and
deepening it. That factor is attitude.
—WILLIAM JAMES

To disagree, one doesn't have to be disagreeable.
—BARRY GOLDWATER

There is perhaps no situation in which the words *with all due respect* are more pertinent, and indispensable, than in matters of disagreement. Conflict is an inherent part of life, in virtually every arena—among individuals, families, businesses, governments, and countries. As a result, the ability to disagree respectfully is essential for getting along and negotiating with other people, as well as building consensus and compromise.

The act of disagreeing is not the problem per se; it's the manner in which it is conducted that exacerbates tensions. Because the very nature of conflict is to be at odds with an opposing party, discussion and debate are often ripe for and rife with incivility, impeding resolution of the issue at hand. Too often, the exchange devolves into an argument over who is right and who is wrong, or an attack on a person and his beliefs rather than the matter in question. This leads to personal assaults, the erosion of relationships, and no viable solutions.

Just imagine how different life would be if each of us learned to disagree in a respectful manner—less acrimony, fewer bruised feelings, and lower levels of stress; greater insight, understanding, harmony, and efficiency; greater productivity; increased chances to build consensus, alliances, and compromise; a platform to support potential solutions; diminished belligerence and warmongering; and more opportunities for peaceful exchange. Sounds like a dream, doesn't it? Well, it can be real. While your efforts may not result in world peace, you can effect changes with people in your inner circle, beginning with those living under your roof. But first, you have to start with yourself.

To begin, before you are enmeshed in any conflict, it helps to honestly examine your mind-set and motivations: Are you genuinely prepared to discuss points of view and alternatives with a willingness to compromise, or are you on a crusade to win at all costs? Do you want to thoughtfully air and resolve an issue, or do you want to crush the other party? The answer to those questions may determine whether or not you intend or will be able to disagree respectfully. Beyond that, there are some other strategies that can help keep any discussion on track, avoiding polarizing paralysis.

> Just as war is freedom's cost, disagreement is freedom's privilege.
>
> —PRESIDENT BILL CLINTON

Earlier, we talked about tone, which expresses how you *feel* about an issue (and the other person's point of view) as well as your *attitude*. Better to keep your emotions and attitude in check and out of the discussion. Remember that you can say almost *anything*—however disagreeable—if you use a neutral tone. Also, give up the need to be right. Not only may you not be, but that attitude will set a contentious and self-righteous tone and get in the way of opportunities to comprise. To that end, have an open mind and be willing to listen to a different point of view; you may actually learn something.

Keep the discussion fact-based and resolve to aim your remarks above, not below the belt—no name-calling, labeling, or dirty tricks. Avoid making inflammatory remarks designed to incite the other person's emotion and derail the issue at hand. By the same token, when incendiary statements are hurled at you from the other side, resist the temptation to take the bait—hard, I know, but make the effort. When tempers do rise, remember the advice of Archbishop Desmond Tutu, who said, "Don't raise your voice. Improve your argument." Above all, refrain from demonizing the opponent. Don't distort facts or twist the other party's words; in short, that makes you a liar.

Bear in mind that your nonverbal communication—facial expressions and body language—can telegraph attitudes and speak louder than words. While your words may be smooth and soothing, if delivered with a mocking tone and sneering face, you might as well have hurled a stone.

While I've said that it's best to keep emotions restrained in order to focus on the issue at hand, sometimes they also cannot be ignored because they will find a way to leak into and permeate the discussion. When a discussion does threaten to be derailed, in order to get it back on track, the authors of *Difficult Conversations: How to Discuss What Matters Most* suggest various tactics. One is to *reframe*, turning destructive statements into helpful ones and concentrating on the source of the disagreement rather than blaming the other person. They also write, "Listening is not only the skill that lets you into the other person's world; it is also the single most powerful move you can make to keep the conversation constructive." As an example, consider the following exchange between a mother and her son, in which the mother continually reframes the discussion:

MOTHER: The next time you have a term paper, it might be a good idea to begin your research earlier, rather than waiting until the last minute.

SON: You're always criticizing me!

MOTHER: I'm sure that there are times when you hear my remarks as critical; however, I'm offering a suggestion that might alleviate your stress when it comes to homework deadlines.

SON: Nothing I do is ever right or makes you happy.

MOTHER: You know that isn't true. As your parent, however, it is my job to offer guidance that may help you in school now, and in college later on.

SON: So that's why you don't let me drive the car when I need it! You think I'm irresponsible and don't spend enough time studying!

MOTHER: I'm encouraging you to develop better organization skills that will be useful to you in all areas of your life. Perhaps you can suggest other ways to accomplish that goal.

SON: (*finally shifting toward responsibility*) Well, maybe I could do my homework before I go on Facebook.

In this short space, I can't detail all the processes and ways that disagreements catapult an issue off the table rather than resolving it, nor are there guaranteed solutions to every disagreement. Certainly, it helps to remain calm, without becoming defensive in the process, because no one listens when that occurs. However, when no consensus can be reached, respectfully *agree to disagree*. Even among the closest associates, some topics are too divisive to pursue. Your position may not be worth destroying a relationship over, particularly one that is otherwise beneficial and worth preserving. Also, if it is apparent that the other party genuinely has no knowledge of the subject matter, but cherishes rage, it might be better to back off. Recalling U.S. senator and statesman William G. McAdoo, "It is impossible to defeat an ignorant man in an argument."

Ultimately, our willingness and commitment as individuals to being open in order to solve a problem is foremost; resolution has to be more important than our desire to be the top dog or to have our own way or opinion prevail.

Remember that disagreement is a normal part of life; our agility and skill in disagreeing respectfully can make all the difference in how we connect with one another—or not—as individuals, communities, and countries. We have the strength and power to rise above, rather than blame, the limitations of human nature.

❧ 14 ❧

Keep a Negotiation on Track

During a negotiation, it would be wise not to take
anything personally. If you leave personalities out of it,
you will be able to see opportunities more objectively.
—BRIAN KOSLOW

etting to Yes, by Roger Fisher and William Ury, is a book that emerged
out of the Harvard Negotiation Project, an endeavor committed to
negotiation, problem solving, and dispute resolution. The authors posit
that negotiations can take place more smoothly when both sides work
jointly, focusing on common interests rather than arguing over individual
positions, leaving adversarial posturing by the wayside. While what has
become known as the Harvard Method is employed as a means to resolve
problems between governments and businesses, the principles can be
equally useful among individuals. As part of the process, the authors suggest, for instance, that any negotiation be a principled one, based on its
own merits, and composed of four elements:

1. *"Separate the people from the problem,"* a tactic intended to minimize
   human emotions and egos that can interfere in resolving conflicts.

2. *"Focus on interests, not positions,"* so that the underlying issues are
   addressed and effectively dealt with, rather than engaging in any
   posturing.

3. *"Generate a variety of possibilities before deciding what to do"*; that is, create a list of potential solutions that are mutually beneficial, formulated
   in advance rather than during the heat and pressure of the moment.

4. *"Insist that the result be based on some objective standard,"* such as fair market value, an expert opinion, or a law.

Human beings, however, are complex creatures who are subject to our emotions, egos, opinions, beliefs, and vested interests. Without an outside arbiter on hand, coupled with self-restraint and a firm set of rules by which we are willing to abide, we frequently tumble off the wagon, falling short of our ideals and goals. Nevertheless, let's attempt to apply this four-step process to the simple scenario below.

Jack and Stephen are employees of the ABC Company. Both are strong leaders, with Jack as head of sales and Stephen the director of accounting. Jack, who is somewhat overbearing, has more power and influence, because he drives the company's revenue. Stephen, a numbers guy, considers Jack a spendthrift. The issue on the table is how to grow the bottom line in a volatile economy. Jack's solution is to add costly sales personnel, a tactic with no guaranteed results, whereas Stephen is more cautious.

As the negotiation begins, Jack boasts that he has the CEO on his side. Though shaken, Stephen keeps his bruised ego in check. Employing rule number one, he suggests that raising revenue should be the focus, which will ultimately please the CEO. As the exchange progresses, tension builds as each man contemplates whether his department will lose influence should the other one have the winning strategy. Although maintaining power is seductive, Stephen contemplates the consequences if no viable solution is reached. Moving on to rule number two, he stays on course by concentrating on the negotiation.

Before the meeting, Jack and Stephen each studied cost-effective and less risky options that could be employed—step three. For instance, the sales force could be increased gradually rather than all at once; the product line could be expanded and diversified; the company could employ e-commerce strategies; or an additional demographic could be targeted. Ultimately, in step four, Jack and Steve understood that the CEO would make the final decision.

This obviously is an oversimplification of a complex process, which is spelled out in much greater detail in *Getting to Yes*. Nonetheless, these are elements that can be a part of any negotiation, even when implemented unilaterally, where egos, emotions, and divergent opinions threaten to lead to disagreement and a breakdown in communication. What makes this process work, however, is that it focuses on the issues and the facts; if you want to keep a negotiation on track, assaulting the other party because you don't like his or her opinions or ideas never works.

Don't Burn Bridges

The only bad thing about burning your bridges
behind you is that the world is round.
—ANONYMOUS

I learned a valuable lesson many years ago, which I will relay in a narra-
tive that I refer to as the "Sally Story."

My friend Tom, who later became my husband, and I were invited to
his boss's house for dinner; the next-door neighbors, Sally and Ed, were
invited, too. It was in the midst of a divisive presidential campaign, and
after consuming a couple of glasses of wine, we foolishly began to discuss
that election. As the exchange of views became more heated, Sally stood
up and, walking over to the chair where I was sitting, leaned over, and
disapprovingly shook her finger in my face. "If you vote for that ******
for president," she exclaimed to me, "you'll be selling this country down
the road!"

Stunned, as well as shaken, by Sally's ferocity, I excused myself to pow-
der my nose. Fortunately, by the time I returned to the dinner table, the
conversation had moved on to a less controversial topic.

At the end of the evening, as she was about to depart, Sally looked at me
and said, "I just loved meetin' you!" Shocked beyond belief, I muttered a
reciprocal sort of parting compliment. On the way home, however, I
became unstitched over the incident, incensed by Sally's, in my estimation,
hypocritical sweet good-bye after she had so vociferously challenged me
earlier. I talked about Sally for weeks, even months, unable to shake her
insincere posturing. I couldn't imagine how she could—or why she
would—ever make such a hypocritical comment!

Decades later I recalled that turbulent evening and suddenly realized that Sally had actually taught me an extraordinarily valuable lesson in civility. For if we ever saw each other on the street after that night, we could be polite and say hello. Were we ever to work together in a business or volunteer arena, we would more readily be able to develop a respectful relationship. And if we, again, ever found ourselves sitting across the table from one another at a dinner party, we could carry on a pleasant conversation.

In a sense, Sally's parting words were a sort of peace offering that would enable us to go forward and remain mutually civil when in the same company.

I often use the Sally Story in my seminars to drive home the following point to my students: Don't burn bridges. Keep the lines of communication open. Regardless of the volatility of a discussion, begin and

> He who burns his bridges better be a damn good swimmer.
>
> —ANONYMOUS

end the meeting with a handshake so that both sides can keep talking. Refrain from drawing divisive lines in the sand. Being respectful and polite may be your best tool in business relationships, as well as social ones. Always leave the line open so that dialogue can continue—with your spouse, your children, your friends, and your colleagues. Part politely!

Ordinarily, I would not advocate dwelling on unpleasantness. In this instance, however, I'm glad that I did so, because it became one of the most worthwhile lessons that I ever learned. And I give Sally full credit for teaching it to me.

16

Set Your Moral Compass

There can be no high civility without a deep morality.
—RALPH WALDO EMERSON

When I do good, I feel good.
When I do bad, I feel bad. That's my religion.
—ABRAHAM LINCOLN

Civility is related to ethics, which is defined by *Webster's Dictionary* as "the system or code of morals of a particular person, religion, group, or profession." Rules of civility exist, in part, because they provide a structure to society, averting chaos, so that we all don't run amok, serving our own self-interest and quest for gratification. However, those rules are behavioral guidelines, not laws; we uphold and abide by them voluntarily because we choose to, not because we are forced to. While our reason for conforming may be related to our desire to avoid society's disapproval, we also do so because our internal voice tells us that it's the right thing to do. That judgment of what is right and wrong comes from our sense of morality. Thus, civility goes hand in hand with morality.

Polite and civilized behavior requires us to respect and treat every human being well, as we would like to be treated—the creed of the golden rule. While morality underlies civility, it also undergirds our ability to cooperate with others. Throughout evolution, research tells us, morality has been a critical factor in binding groups together. Upholding group norms increased solidarity as well as cohesion and trust, and the establishment of moral communities often enabled groups to achieve goals that individuals were not able to attain by themselves. Cooperation not only served as an important means of survival among members of a group but also was an expedient factor in opposing outside groups. It aided the suppression of selfishness and made social life possible. Personal reputation and punishment—even through shame or gossip—were integral to the system. What others thought of an individual enhanced or detracted from her standing within the group, corrective elements that are often less influential in our present culture.

> Morality is of the highest importance— but for us, not for God.
>
> —ALBERT EINSTEIN

When our morality stems from deeply rooted and ingrained values, doing the right thing becomes automatic, without question or hesitation. Our moral compass shapes and guides our thinking about what it means to be part of a community and how we bear responsibility for our friends, colleagues, and neighbors. When a need presents itself, whether it is responding to a disastrous earthquake or tsunami or standing up for human rights, our sense of caring is piqued so that our response is instinctual and spontaneous.

That same sense of morality applies to our daily interactions. You are inclusive of people in a group, not only because you are polite, but also because it is the right thing to do. At a company banquet, you don't take more than your share, not only because it's bad etiquette, but also because you care that others are fed, too. You teach your children manners so that they will be successful, but also because respecting and appreciating others makes the world a better place.

Civility urges us to respect and treat others well; our morality strengthens the bonds of human connection, so that we, in our actions, embrace humankind.

~ 17 ~

Build Trust

We're never so vulnerable than when we trust
someone—but paradoxically, if we cannot trust,
neither can we find love or joy.
—WALTER ANDERSON

In the Galapagos Islands, it is known that turtles and other sea life swim alongside humans, making eye contact, because they have no fear of us. Instinctively, humans do not have that same level of trust toward one another. Through facial expression and body language, early humans learned to observe signals that triggered a fight-or-flight response, depending on how they judged the safety of an oncoming person. Beyond that initial reaction, we are each obliged to peel back the layers to determine whether we feel safe with others—as they do with us. We engage in a dance that can endure for minutes or even years to discover a person's trustworthiness, discerning if he intends to harm us—or not. Our comfort level will influence whether we want to know or associate with someone, as well as how much we reveal of ourselves in the process. Obviously, others are likewise sizing us up simultaneously, judging whether we have their best interests at heart or are undermining them.

It is impossible to have any meaningful relationship if there is no trust. Thus, along with respect, trust becomes a crucial ingredient in developing and deepening our relationships with others. To clarify, I'm not talking about creating a false or manipulated sense of trust, as pedophiles do when preying on children. I'm referring to traits and interactive behaviors that let others know that they are safe with us. While we cannot control how other people think, feel, or behave, there are things that we can do to create an atmosphere where their trust in us can build.

Trust means that you will not harm another, physically or emotionally. Verbal abuse, distorting the meaning of someone's words, unconstructive criticism, or using language designed to embarrass someone in public destroys trust. Your loyalty to a person, not merely fidelity, but having her back and supporting her interests, is critical in building trust. In so doing, know that you also cannot revert and trample on her with track shoes.

People must trust your authenticity, that you are who you say you are, that you're not Machiavellian, with underlying motives. Do you say what you mean and mean what you say, or are you insincere and disingenuous with your words, creating disbelief, as politicians are often accused of being? Are you genuine in your comments about others, or are you two-faced, saying one thing to a person's face and another behind her back? Your honesty, but not brutality, in your words, is equally important. Honesty also implies that you will not, like a thief, steal a person's belongings—or spouse!—nor cheat anyone out of anything that rightfully belongs to her, whether it is an idea, credit for work, or winnings in a poker game. Know that undermining another's credible reputation in order to boost yours is simply another means of stealing. Further, can you be counted on to do what you say you will do—be it a task or showing up on time—or is your reliability in question? If you make a promise to me, will you uphold it, or if I tell you a secret, can I trust that you will keep it? Can I be assured that you will neither misrepresent me nor twist my words, distorting my meaning?

> A man who doesn't trust himself can never really trust anyone else.
>
> —JEAN FRANÇOIS PAUL DE GONDI, CARDINAL DE RETZ

Trust plays a critical role in our society and in our ability to cooperate. Your trustworthiness in business will determine your ability to sustain long-term relationships, as a supplier delivering the goods, or as a client who pays on a timely basis. As an employer, your trust in your employees and customers will affect their trust in you. Trust created in a courtroom may well determine whether a defendant is declared innocent or guilty, and trust between a doctor and patient may affect how a patient proceeds with treatment and even the rate of recovery. Our trust in our officials, authority figures, and government has a profound effect on what we believe and the strength of our institutions.

There are innumerable other factors that build or destroy trust, and the deeper we progress in our relationships, peeling back the layers, the more vulnerable we become, as the stakes are raised. How much we decide to reveal ourselves is a personal decision. If we want to deepen our relationships, however, it is incumbent on us to *earn* that trust from others. If we ourselves want to grow into the fullness of life, we must also *learn* to trust, taking a risk by exposing our vulnerability. Trust builds bonds between people and society; in short, we must have a basic level of trust in order to function and survive.

Trust, according to University of Frankfurt business professor Michael Kosfeld, is "one of the distinguishing features of the human species. An element of trust characterizes almost all human social interactions. When trust is absent, we are, in a sense, dehumanized."

Strive for Truth

If you tell the truth you don't have to remember anything.

—MARK TWAIN

A truth that's told with bad intent
beats all the lies you can invent.

—WILLIAM BLAKE

The original title of this chapter was "Tell the Truth"; however, I soon realized that this was not a universal missive, because there are times when there are valid reasons not to tell the truth, or the whole truth. For example, one way to lie is by deliberately omitting facts or withholding information. Yet, in some legal situations, it is *illegal* to divulge everything you know. There are other circumstances where telling a lie is a just and moral response, as when Christians who hid Jews from the Nazis denied knowledge of the Jews' whereabouts. So difficult is the determination of what lying is, and why it is okay to lie in some instances but not in others, that theologians have wrestled with this moral question for centuries, without concrete answers.

A few years back, screenwriter, advertising copywriter, and book author Stephanie Ericsson penned a well-known, thought-provoking essay titled "The Way We Lie," in which she depicted ten different ways that we bend the truth. According to Ms. Ericsson, *Webster's Dictionary's* definition of a *lie* provides vast wiggle room for many more types of lies than the ten she presented:

The cruelest lies are often told in silence.

—ADLAI STEVENSON

1. A false statement or action especially made with the intent to deceive

2. Anything that gives or is meant to give a false impression

Ms. Ericsson suggests that lying is so prevalent in our culture that it is almost impossible not to lie. She first refers to the little *white lie*, which we all employ because we wish to avoid hurting a friend's feelings when she asks how we like her new, albeit unflattering, hairdo. Or, when we are twenty minutes late for an appointment and fib that we were delayed by traffic when, in truth, we left our house twenty minutes later than we should have. Or, when we don't wish to have a protracted argument with an irrational three-year-old who doesn't need but wants cookies, so we tell him that there are none. While we all fall prey to this form of untruth, we should, nonetheless, bear in mind the words of American writer Austin O'Malley, "Those who think it is permissible to tell white lies soon grow color-blind," lest it become a too convenient and frequent response.

Prevaricate. Equivocate. Fabricate. Omit. Obstruct. Sugarcoat. Spin. Distort. Delude. Mislead. And so on. We do not enumerate all the multiple strategies for lying when we teach our children—quite simply—to never tell a lie, to always tell the truth. We point to George Washington and the tale of his fallen cherry tree as a shining example. By the time we reach adulthood, however, we've come not only to accept but also to expect ubiquitous deception as part of our society. *Webster's* definition does not state whether it is right or wrong to deceive. However, there are times when it is profoundly wrong to lie, times when the truth should and must be told—unequivocally, in full. As a way of delineating those situations, and supplying a bit of moral undergirding, I would like to add to *Webster's* definition, when there is *intentional harm* toward the other party, or a *harmful outcome* results, due to the deception.

> A half-truth is a whole lie.
>
> —YIDDISH PROVERB

Okay, you and I can already think of ways to get around that one, because we're armed and ready to tell our enemy, who is about to shoot us, that our own gun is not loaded when, in truth, it really is. However, what I am aiming for here is to point to our need, as individuals, and as a society, for transparency and truth. For without truth, there can be no trust.

Without trust, we have no way to bind our relationships with one another, no way to bind our society together. Truth and trust, thus, become foundational to the way that we function and live.

We need to believe our children, our spouses, our doctors, and what we read in the newspapers. Without truth, or at least *striving* for truth, we cannot trust our business community, our election process, our elected officials, or our government. Truth and trust go hand in hand.

Striving for the truth, thus, is pivotal to our community, locally and globally. Rather than figuring out all the ways to lie and justify our deceit, we should all be looking for ways to tell the truth—without apology.

❧ 19 ❧

Take the High Road

The high road is always respected.
Honesty and integrity are always rewarded.
—SCOTT HAMILTON

In our popular culture today, the high road is undoubtedly becoming one that is less frequently traveled. For those unfamiliar with the expression, it does not refer to a psychedelic journey or illegal drugs, but rather pertains to behavior that is ultimately dignified and decent, not always visible in these contemporary times.

John C. Maxwell, Christian minister and prolific author of books on leadership, describes three roads we can travel through life: the low road, where we treat people worse than they treat us; the middle road, where we treat people the same as they treat us; and the high road, where we treat people better than they treat us.

Few of us are likely to admit to taking the low road where we readily trod on others, especially if they have been nice to us. There are also negative implications to the second route in that we treat others *only* as nicely as they treat us. That says little about our ability to elevate our standards of behavior or set a positive tone. The bar is raised, however, when we follow that third route, in which we refuse to respond in negative fashion to the taunts, criticism, meanness, or pettiness of those who may use such measures to attack or undermine us. In taking the high road, we not only rise above the fray but, in fact, turn the other cheek, which sometimes has the effect of turning the tables on our opponents. Abraham Lincoln once said, "I destroy my enemies when I make them my friends." Immense patience, inner strength, and equanimity are required in order to act with such dignity, decency, and decorum; that, my friends, is called character.

Taking the high road is a principled course based on ethics and integrity. The term *ethics* is derived from the Greek word *ethos*, which forms the root of *ethikos*, meaning character. *Integrity*, as a concept of ethics, refers to the truthfulness and honesty of our actions, based on our discernment of right and wrong. It stems from the Latin word *integer*, which means whole, complete, and unified. To have integrity, therefore, implies that you behave in a manner that is consistent with your internal principles and beliefs.

The high road, however, is not always an easy one; it is challenging, and sometimes we stumble, in both our personal and our public lives. It is not an easy task to always make the right decision based on what's right, or to do the right thing because it's the right thing to do. We get caught up in the drama of life and often respond with the same bad behavior of which we accuse others. Our own complicity comes when we volley with insults and rudeness or other destructive responses. In a climate of polarized politics, we strike back with slings and arrows at the other side that riled us. Tit for tat does nothing to advance a discussion or resolve a problem, just as a fire will never be extinguished by fanning the flames. As Gandhi once observed, "An eye for an eye only makes the whole world blind." When you are wronged, you don't have to be silent or nonresponsive. Rather than swallowing bait by lashing out in retaliation, let your reply be dignified. That requires thoughtfulness and restraint. It also takes character.

There is something even more valuable to civilization than wisdom, and that is character.

—H. L. MENCKEN

20

Laugh at Least
Once a Day

I love people who make me laugh.
I honestly think it's the thing I like most, to laugh.
It cures a multitude of ills. It's probably
the most important thing in a person.
—AUDREY HEPBURN

Laughter is an instant vacation.
—MILTON BERLE

Knock, knock!
Who's there?
Little old lady.
Little old lady who?
I didn't know you could yodel!

Did you happen to laugh at that little joke? If not, you might believe such rib-ticklers were only funny during your childhood days. Science tells us, however, that there could be other reasons why the joke failed to elicit a laugh—one of which is that you're sitting there reading it by yourself rather than potentially chuckling over it with a group of people. According to research, we are thirty times more apt to laugh when in the company of others than when we are by ourselves. Why is that? In part, it's because most laughter has more to do with social factors than with the humor itself. As *New York Times* science columnist John Tierney wrote, "[Laughter is] an instinctual survival tool for social animals.... It's not about getting the joke. It's about getting along." Thus, laughter is a powerful tool for connecting with and relating to other human beings.

University of Maryland psychologist Robert R. Provine, who has studied laughter for more than two decades, actually found that laughter and humor are not inextricably linked, as earlier studies had assumed. He originally began his research in the laboratory, where he would show video clips and then note a participant's reaction; in this setting, Provine discovered that not much laughter occurred. He then moved the camera out into public spaces where he observed 1,200 people and what really happened when they laughed spontaneously in a natural environment. Truly humorous content, as it turned out, produced genuine laughter only 10 to 20 percent of the time.

What surprised Provine, however, was that most laughter occurred in a predialogue stage, whereby the *speaker* was 46 percent more likely to laugh than the listener, and that the lines that preceded the speaker's laughter were ordinary statements like, "Where have you been?" Women, in particular, often used laughter as punctuation for their sentences. Provine also found that when he asked an individual to laugh without provocation, it was a nearly impossible task: Laughter is more of an involuntary response than it is a voluntary one; we often are not even aware of when we are laughing.

Having gained insights into the evolution of laughter through his earlier research on neuromuscular control of laughter and its link to the respiratory systems of humans and chimpanzees, Provine concluded that our laughter is not a learned group reaction but an instinctive and primal behavior, programmed by our genes. "Laughter," he says, "bonds us through humor and play." Laughter, believed by some scientists to have preceded language, likely developed through evolution as a social signal, a declaration that we are ready for friendly interaction. The very sound of the human *ha-ha* laugh is thought to have emerged from the rhythmic *pant-pant* sound that chimpanzees make, particularly when they are being tickled—a laugh-related behavior that they share with *Homo sapiens*. In fact, Provine believes that tickling is at the root of laughter, and that "feigned tickling," much as parents do with babies, may have been the original primate joke. This ritual is a way in which parents and children bond, an early behavior on which we later draw socially as adults. Tickling has an element of surprise to which we respond when we're young, much as we later respond to the surprise twist in a joke. Tickling is also fun: It helps us play well with others. When young mammals play, laughter is how the brain shows that play is pleasurable. But perhaps more than that, Provine believes that it comes from touching and being touched, important parts of being a mammal.

To date, little research has been done that tells us how and why we laugh or exactly why it feels so good. Although it can be used negatively to ridicule others in order to exclude them from a group, laughter is more often a tool that eases social interactions. One study, by neuroscientist Sophie Scott at the University College London, has shown that laughter is truly contagious. The same mirroring behavior, such as smiling, that we often unconsciously do as humans, also seems to apply to laughing, at least at the cerebral level. Scott believes that this automatic response to positive emotions also helps us interact socially. Another study by psychologists at the universities of Kent and Liverpool points to a finding that may link laughter to other prosocial behavior, such as altruism. Participants in a control group that laughed while watching a funny video, as opposed to a group that viewed a serious one, were inclined to give more money to others, a finding that could have future implications for charitable giving.

> Through humor, you can soften some of the worst blows that life delivers. And once you find laughter, no matter how painful your situation might be, you can survive it.
>
> —BILL COSBY

Laughter has also been found to have a positive effect on health and well-being, an area of inquiry since author and journalist Norman Cousins wrote *Anatomy of an Illness*, a book and subsequent made-for-television movie, back in the 1970s. Cousins, who had been diagnosed with an autoimmune disease, chronicled his experience during which he prescribed for himself a daily regimen of high doses of vitamin C and hours of watching outrageously funny Marx Brothers movies. His experience was further documented in the esteemed *New England Journal of Medicine*, in which he reported to have literally belly-laughed himself into remission.

Since that time, Dr. Lee S. Berk, a preventive care specialist and psychoneuroimmunology researcher at Loma Linda's University Schools of Allied Health (SAHP), and his colleague, Dr. Stanley Tan, picked up the mantle, studying the effect of mirthful laughter and its effects on various body systems. They found that laughter decreases levels of cortisol and epinephrine, two hormones linked to stress. In addition to reducing stress and lowering blood pressure, laughter enhances the body's immune activity and mood. The subsequent Laughercise program that they developed has shown that mirthful laughter can be likened to "internal jogging," which produces a benefit similar to repetitive exercise. Laughing makes us breathe more deeply, oxygenating the organs and increasing blood circulation. It also causes the body to release powerful endorphins, those "feel good" hormones. This mild form of exercise has also been reported to have positive effects on the elderly, who sometimes suffer from "wasting disease," whereby they become depressed, accompanied by a loss of appetite and physical activity. As recently as 2010, Berk, along with Loma Linda colleague Dr. Jerry Petrofsky, presented further research showing that laughing can be a tool for getting the elderly back on track.

Ongoing studies will continue to explore the possible links between laughter and health. However, Provine does not believe that laughter evolved through time in order to improve our autoimmune systems, but rather that these are coincidental consequences. The primary goal of laughter has been to bring people together. Rather than responding to humor, we're responding to the connectedness that is a result of infectious laughter.

Although we may not yet be able to prove scientifically what precipitates laughter, that doesn't matter. This is one time that we don't need science to affirm that laughter is good for us; we already know that because it *feels so darned good*! Whatever brings it on, laughter is some of the most fun we'll ever have ... so we might as well lighten our lives and the world and whoop it up as often as possible. *So ...*

> Knock knock!
> Who's there?
> Police.
> Police who?
> Police stop telling these awful knock, knock jokes!

21

Just Be Nice!

Treat everyone with politeness,
even those who are rude to you—
not because they are nice,
but because you are.

—ANONYMOUS

A few years back, one of my friends, downsized from her work, shared her frustrations regarding prospective employers who no longer extend the basic courtesy of acknowledging applicants' job submissions. I empathized with her discontent—hurt, actually—because being ignored in this manner is another way of saying that you don't exist, don't matter, or are beneath someone's attention. The same goes for not returning e-mails or phone calls, or disregarding a person to whom you've just been introduced. It's rude. In fact, it's just not nice.

Happily, I discovered that not every business operates in that fashion. Linda Kaplan Thaler and Robin Koval, co-heads of a billion-dollar advertising firm, acknowledge every application they receive the same day it comes in. Further, they believe so heartily in such behavior that they wrote a book about it called—what else?—*The Power of Nice*. In it, they cite countless examples of how it pays to be nice, likening the energy created by "nice deeds" to sowing positive seeds. You not only make a difference in peoples' lives but may also reap unexpected dividends. While they have a personal and company policy of being polite and considerate to everyone, they mention one instance in which they were nice to Melania Trump, who was featured in one of their commercials. This was duly noted by her famous husband, Donald, who returned the favor by effusively complimenting their agency on his television show *The Apprentice*.

Isn't being nice the same as being kind? Well, yes and no. While both traits involve consideration, a spirit of generosity, and a willingness to help others, I think of kindness differently. Mother Teresa, for instance, didn't live among and love the poor because she was nice, even though she was; she did it out of loving devotion and her kind heart. Niceness, for purposes here, refers more to solicitous consideration.

Being nice means that you treat the mailroom clerk with the same thoughtfulness as you would the CEO, are as polite to a janitor as you are to a customer, and smile as readily at a cashier as you would at Santa Claus. It means that you put yourself on equal footing with every other human being, so that you behave in neither a superior nor an inferior fashion. It means that you check your ego for signs of inflation, so that you don't exaggerate your self-importance or see others as beneath you. Recall celebrities, for instance, who, with humility, recognize their fans rather than fleeing them.

Nice people include others, providing easier entrée into a circle or group. They share, and they don't hog credit for work that involved many hands. They pay attention to and show interest in people, offering compliments and putting in a good word for them, rather than gossiping behind their backs. They are neither disdainful nor condescending.

Being nice also means doing nice things for people in a spirit of "everyone helps." While that help can be an act of kindness or charity, it can be as simple as moving a shopping cart that deters access to a parking spot, opening the door for a mother who is pushing a stroller with a toddler in hand, or allowing the person behind you in a checkout line to go ahead of you when he has only one item. Tiny gestures that take only seconds can make all the difference, to the other person as well as yourself. When you're nice, you not only do good things for others, but you also notice when they do the same for you and express your appreciation.

Being nice also means that you watch your disposition, so that your bad mood precludes your barking or snapping at other people. It is recognizing that cheerfulness can be contagious and welcoming, making you approachable, maybe even charming!

Knowing how to say no appropriately is also part of cultivating niceness. Whether you are a gatekeeper, responsible for shielding your boss, or are guarding state secrets, you don't have to do so in a mean or ugly way. You can be dogged in your efforts without barking like a rottweiler! Nor do you have to be nasty and negative, regardless of your role, in business or other areas of life.

Someone once said, "It is better to be nice to people on your way up, because you may meet them on your way down." Follow that advice, not as protection against a fall, but because it is the nice thing to do.

∞ 22 ∞

Cultivate Optimism

A pessimist sees the difficulty in every opportunity;
an optimist sees the opportunity in every difficulty.
—WINSTON CHURCHILL

I can't change the direction of the wind, but I can
adjust my sails to always reach my destination.
—JIMMY DEAN

One evening an old Cherokee told his grandson about a battle that goes
on inside people. He said, "My son, the battle is between two wolves
inside us all. One is Evil. It is fear, anger, envy, jealousy, sorrow, regret,
greed, arrogance, self-pity, guilt, resentment, inferiority, lies, false pride,
superiority, and ego. The other is Good. It is joy, peace, love, hope, serenity, humility, kindness, benevolence, empathy, generosity, truth, compassion, and faith." The grandson thought for a moment and then asked his
grandfather, "Which wolf wins?" The old Cherokee simply replied, "The
one you feed."

The inherent wisdom of this Native American parable is not about good
versus evil but, rather, intentional choices we make in areas of our lives that
are within our control. One of those areas is whether we choose to be positive or negative in our thoughts, outlook, and relationships. How we look
at the world and what happens to us can be viewed through a lens of optimism or pessimism; the true bright side is that we have an opportunity to
choose our focus. In that sense, we are and become what we think. A positive attitude, coupled with an optimistic vision, provides a strong foundation for a meaningful life, in which you more readily connect with people

and develop fulfilling relationships. Not only does your positive outlook make you more approachable to other people, but it also helps you *see* the best in them and be more likely to extend them the benefit of a doubt.

In *Positivity*, University of North Carolina social psychologist Barbara Fredrickson cites ten emotions that shape our level of positivity: joy, gratitude, serenity, interest, hope, pride, amusement, inspiration, awe, and love. Her extensive research shaped a "broaden and build" theory of positive emotions, whereby an increased level of heartfelt positivity "broadens our minds and hearts" and "builds our resources." Negativity narrows our minds and constricts our thinking so that we see fewer possibilities. Based on hundreds of studies, Fredrickson developed a 3:1 ratio of positive to negative emotions that determines whether we flourish or languish. Our level of positivity helps us not only feel good but also *do* good, allowing us to make a greater contribution to the world. "People who flourish," says Fredrickson, "are highly engaged with their families, work, and communities. They're driven by a sense of purpose: they know why they get up in the morning."

An overwhelming body of scientific studies points to the advantages of optimism over pessimism. Overall, optimists are more successful in school, at work, and in sports; they're better performers on aptitude tests; they generally enjoy better health and live longer; and they are more likely to be elected to public office. They are more resilient in coping with adversity and are able to recover more quickly from setbacks, which they view as temporary obstacles, not crushing defeats. Optimists are more positive in the way that they think about themselves and life's circumstances; they observe and recognize the good things that happen, largely because they *expect* good things to happen. Pessimists, on the other hand, are more prone to depression and give up more easily. They view situations and people with a negative slant, often believing that bad things are always going to happen to them and thinking that a setback is a permanent condition. While optimists envision the possibilities, pessimists focus on the obstacles.

> If you realized how powerful your thoughts are, you would never think a negative thought.
>
> —PEACE PILGRIM

So which are you—an optimist or a pessimist? Consider the following situations, and whether you would respond in a positive or a negative manner:

Situation #1. At a business networking reception, an acquaintance spends most of his time talking to other colleagues, but only a moment with you. A pessimist returns home, sulking over his apparent lack of importance. An optimist doesn't perceive the incident as a slight, and instead assumes that his acquaintance was networking for a new job.

Situation #2. Two weeks before the wedding, a groom tells his bride-to-be that he no longer wants to marry her. A pessimistic bride is crestfallen, becomes depressed, no longer pursues other relationships, and gives up on any future plans to marry. An optimistic bride, after taking time to heal her wounds, decides that there must be a good reason for the breakup, which fortunately occurred before the wedding, rather than after. She begins dating again, marries a wonderful man, and has a meaningful life.

Situation #3. A boss says to her employee that she has been observing his work of late and would like to have a word with him at the end of the day. A pessimist begins wringing his hands, wondering what he has done wrong and fearful that he might be about to lose his job. An optimist thinks about how he has demonstrated his capabilities, which might be leading to his appointment to spearhead a division. He also looks forward to the meeting to discuss his fresh new ideas.

Situation #4. A premed college student receives a poor grade on a biochemistry final exam. A pessimist loses confidence about getting into medical school, feeling doomed to a life of failure. An optimist looks at the grade as a wake-up call and investigates additional study aids. He recognizes that he needs to study more intensely, and perhaps take a course or two over the summer.

While the above scenarios are obvious and elementary, they illustrate the point that how you perceive events in your life will often determine their outcomes. Dr. Martin Seligman, a known expert on "learned optimism" and "learned helplessness," is also a founder—along with his colleague, psychologist Mihaly Csikszentmihalyi—of positive psychology, a recognized discipline that focuses on what makes people thrive and be happy. The University of Pennsylvania Center for Authentic Happiness offers online questionnaires that assess your optimism, as well as other levels of emotion, engagement, life meaning, and satisfaction. Simply log on to www.authentichappiness.com and create a profile; the self-directed online tests are free of charge.

Similarly, using Barbara Fredrickson's website (www.PositivityRatio.com), you can track your positive-to-negative ratio. No matter what your age, it is never too late to learn ways to cultivate the important attribute of a positive attitude.

Whether you go through life as an optimist or a pessimist, your attitude has enormous implications, affecting individual happiness, success, health, and your connection to other people. As stated earlier, however, you can *learn* to be more optimistic, largely by being aware of your thoughts and refuting the negative ones. Misfortunes can be viewed either as debilitating or as opportunities for growth. You can dwell on the good or the bad—it's your choice.

23

Embrace Kindness

Three things in human life are important. The first is to
be kind. The second is to be kind. The third is to be kind.
—HENRY JAMES

No act of kindness, no matter how small, is ever wasted.
—AESOP

Just be kind. It's a short directive and astonishingly simple. As an adjective, *kind* embodies that which is benevolent, loving, and considerate. One of the seven heavenly virtues, *kindness* encompasses charity, generosity, compassion, and empathy. As it applies to good behavior, it is a nearly inclusive antidote to disrespect, inconsideration, and rudeness. If we simply were kind to everyone, a host of other negative behaviors would fall by the wayside.

Think about it ... generous in our thoughts, we would automatically think well of others, giving them the benefit of the doubt. Our words would be soft and well chosen, not sharp or abusive, and our actions would be gentle. We would be tolerant and accepting of others. And in performing random acts of kindness, we would do good toward others but reap the benefit of our own good feelings as well.

Being kind sounds effortless, but it is not. As described above, kindness sounds almost impossible, like behavior attainable only by the likes of a beatified human being such as Mother Teresa, not by lesser mortals like ourselves, who consistently fall short. There are ordinary people, however, who may not be as renowned as Mother Teresa, but who set examples for us every day. Fortunately, I was blessed to know one, my great-aunt Esta, who was undoubtedly the gentlest person I've ever known. Growing up, I spent a week every summer on her farm, along with three other little cousins who, like me, were persnickety and quarrelsome little girls.

During all those years, I never saw my aunt's face without a soft smile, in spite of numerous sources of aggravation. Although she and my uncle lived on a shoestring, Aunt Esta nonetheless set a bountiful table. And when disputes occurred between her four churlish houseguests, which happened often, she neither reprimanded nor took sides; instead, she gave each of us a warm hug and a pat on the cheek. Never even acknowledging our whining, she let her sweetness actually nip it in the bud! In the fifty-plus years that I knew her, not once did I hear her utter an unkind word about anything or anybody; she always maintained the same even temperament.

The example of my aunt Esta is intended to show that you don't have to be totally selfless and self-sacrificing, or on a track toward sainthood, in order to be kind and good to others. Nor must you be a milquetoast or lacking in intelligence and discernment. It is also possible to be kind and good without being a doormat or a pushover. For, as renowned Lebanese poet Kahlil Gibran wrote, "Tenderness and kindness are not signs of weakness and despair but manifestations of strength and resolution." As such, kindness—in thought, word, and deed—is *intentional* behavior, requiring commitment as well as discipline and self-restraint. By the same token, we don't have to make the process difficult.

> Kindness in words creates confidence. Kindness in thinking creates profoundness. Kindness in giving creates love.
>
> —LAO TZU

The benefits of kind behavior don't accrue only to the recipient. After scientifically studying happiness for more than eighteen years, Dr. Sonja Lyubomirsky, professor of psychology at the University of California, Riverside, has determined that, despite genetics and environmental circumstances, we control up to 40 percent of our happiness level. In her book *The How of Happiness*, she lists twelve strategies for attaining that goal, one of which is practicing acts of kindness toward others. This leads us "to perceive others more positively and charitably." Further, she reveals a body of scientific evidence that shows that acting kindly can diminish depression, leading to a "helper's high."

These acts do not have to be monumental endeavors or sacrifices in order to qualify as "kind." It isn't necessary, for example, to make dinner for a sick friend every night for a year, pay someone's monthly mortgage, or give away your season tickets for major league baseball. Instead, try fixing dinner one night for your friend or driving your uncle to the doctor. Other simple gestures might be as small as smiling at a stranger or spending a few minutes listening to someone you know is lonely. The rewards of this habitual practice may be priceless. As Dr. Lyubomirsky, among others, points out, small acts like these not only make other people feel good, but they can also precipitate a ripple effect: Those folks are inclined to do the same thing, paying it forward, which is the way life ought to be.

24

Live Generously

We make a living by what we get,
but we make a life by what we give.
—WINSTON CHURCHILL

Do all the good you can,
By all the means you can,
In all the ways you can,
In all the places you can,
At all the times you can,
To all the people you can,
As long as ever you can.
—JOHN WESLEY

The late billionaire and philanthropist Sir John Templeton endowed philanthropic foundations to study how science relates to the "big questions" of love, purpose, spirituality, and creativity. Two such grants funded the Science of Generosity Project at Notre Dame and the Institute for Research on Unlimited Love (IRUL) in Cleveland. Both of these organizations focus on generosity, researching the human effects of giving, including the causes, manifestations, and consequences.

The project at Notre Dame defines generosity as "giving good things to others freely and abundantly," both in attitude and in action. The intent of generosity is to enhance the well-being of others through goodness, but also by eschewing "selfishness, greed, fear, [and] meanness."

Philanthropy plays a crucial role in our society, locally and globally, providing funding and assistance without which many nonprofit organizations, institutions, and even countries would be unable to survive, much less flourish. Measured against this very large form of giving, we, as individuals, often feel small, believing that there is little that we can do to make a difference; however, we are often unaware of the impact of our seemingly small acts. Think, for instance, of times when you have been moved by a simple touch or caring gesture, perhaps from a stranger, whose giving made all the difference in your day. Reflect on moments when you were grateful that you were included as part of a group of which you were not a member, or when a friend gave you a hug because you were having a bad day. We all benefit from that spirit of generosity every day, through the gifts that we receive as well as give.

In his book *Why Good Things Happen to Good People*, Dr. Stephen Post, director of the IRUL and professor of medical ethics at Case Western Reserve, considers *giving* to be the single most potent force on the planet. Neither he nor the project at Notre Dame limits *giving* to a state of pure altruism, whereby the giver has no expectation of receiving anything in return. Instead, Dr. Post refers to the results of more than five hundred scientific studies conducted over the past ten to fifteen years that "demonstrate the power of unselfish love to enhance health" for the giver. Among the extraordinary benefits, he reports that:

- Giving that begins as early as high school is a predictor of good physical and mental health that lasts more than fifty years, well into late adulthood.

- Giving is a factor in reducing adolescent depression and suicide risk.

- Giving has a more powerful positive impact on the givers than on the receivers in terms of reducing mortality.

- Giving helps us forgive ourselves for our own mistakes, an important factor in our well-being.

- Even the act of praying for others reduces the impact of health problems in old age.

Dr. Post, in the same book, categorizes ten different ways in which giving can be manifested. In addition to gratitude, forgiveness, humor, respect, compassion, courage, and listening as areas of giving, Dr. Post describes loyalty, creativity, and *generativity*, which he likens to planting another's garden, the fruits of which continue to blossom and benefit future generations. As such, the receiver *pays forward* nurturing gifts that create a more permanent ripple effect.

In all the major religions of the world, generosity or charity plays an important role. While financial contributions are one aspect, generosity, in religion, encompasses a broader definition, one that includes the virtue of hospitality. For example, the people of the Middle East are known for their abundant hospitality and welcoming of guests, a tradition that comes from the tenet that it is our duty to God to offer the best that we have—in terms of food, drink, and shelter—to strangers. In the Hebrew Bible, Abraham is living in a tent in the wilderness when he is approached by three strangers, who, according to the text, are symbolic of God. Abraham honors God by extending hospitality to these strangers; afterward, despite his advanced age, he is promised a son. Generosity is also a central theme in Christianity, not only in Christ's teachings of giving and taking care of the meek and poor, but also especially in the gift of the Divine Parent: "For God so loved the world that He gave His only begotten Son, that whoever believes in him should not perish but have everlasting life" (John 3:16).

Besides religious tradition, what is it exactly that makes us want to give? What makes us open our hearts and consider another's needs before our own? When a natural disaster hits—a tsunami in Indonesia or an earthquake in Haiti—why are we inspired and compelled to pull out our checkbooks and donate money to help people we don't even know? In recent years, researchers have been probing the new neuroscience of generosity, looking for clues to why we give and also why some give more freely than others. *New York Times* columnist Nicholas D. Kristof wrote about the research of Dr. Jorge Moll of the National Institutes of Health. Brain scans of participants in Moll's research showed that areas of the brain that are usually associated with human pleasures, like eating and sex, lit up when the subjects were even encouraged to think of giving money to a charity. The implication of this is that our brains may be hardwired to give, perhaps because it feels so good to be generous. In her work at the University of Michigan, psychologist Stephanie Brown suggests that one reason that giving shows such positive outcomes is that it makes us feel more connected to others. Given all the studies that point to social relationships as being the number-one predictor of our happiness, her hypothesis certainly seems plausible.

Dr. Paul Zak, the founding director of the Center for Neuroeconomics Studies at Claremont Graduate University, has been studying possible biological motivations behind our desire to give. In particular, he has been researching the effects of oxytocin, a hormone that is known to induce childbirth and lactation, lower blood pressure, and promote social friendliness and bonding between spouses and children. Sometimes known as the "cuddle chemical," oxytocin can often be self-activated through touch, exercise, sexual intimacy, and eye contact. Building on earlier research in which Zak linked higher levels of oxytocin to the potential development of trust among individuals, he began to design experiments to explore how it also might influence our generosity.

In his experiment, which he called the "Generosity Game," Zak randomly assigned groups of two partners. One subject was given ten dollars and instructed to offer a portion of the money to the other subject, who was not shown or introduced to the first subject. (Communication occurred via computers.) The point was for the giver to think about how much the other person needed. If the second participant turned down the offer for any reason, neither walked out of the lab with any money. When the subjects were administered a nasal spray containing oxytocin, they were 80 percent more generous in the amount of money they offered. Although the first subjects had less money at the end of the experiment, they were not necessarily unhappy. Says Zak, "The reason we are charitable is that we can't help it, we have a built-in brain mechanism that connects us to other people." Stephanie Brown refers to this brain mechanism as the "care giving system."

Additional experiments that Zak conducted two years later demonstrated that people were more inclined to give generously when they understood the perspective of the people to whom they were giving, suggesting a link between generosity and empathy. In one study, two videos were shown of a father with his young son—the son was bald due to chemotherapy for treatment of his cancer. In the first video, the father talked about what it was like to know that his son was dying. The second video showed the same father and son at the zoo without any mention of cancer or dying. The emotional response, which made grown men cry, was much more heightened among those who viewed the first video as opposed to the second one. When blood levels were drawn afterward, there was a 157 percent spike in the oxytocin levels of the first group. Zak contends that "oxytocin connects us to others and lets us understand their emotions."

Much more research needs to be done on the neuroscience of giving: We don't yet know why our patterns are so varied, or why some people give much more or much less than others. However, substantive scientific evidence on health and other benefits of giving encourages us to continue to do so; it is also the right thing to do. Generosity not only makes us happier and connects us to others, but it also makes a lasting difference in our lives and theirs. We give, both to strangers and to those we know, because we want to make the world a better place. It also allows us to move beyond our limited concerns and focus on the needs of others. As the late Reverend Bill Coffin, the chaplain at Yale, once said, "Love measures our stature: the more we love, the bigger we are. There is no smaller package in all the world than of a man all wrapped up in himself." Our outer-focus and empathy toward others is a way that we affirm our interconnected humanity, helping us to create a more civilized society and a politer planet.

25

Practice Gratitude

Let us rise up and be thankful, for if we
didn't learn a lot today, at least we learned a little,
and if we didn't learn a little, at least we didn't get
sick, and if we got sick, at least we didn't die;
so, let us all be thankful.
—BUDDHA

Gratitude is an acknowledgment of the goodness in our life and an expression of deep appreciation for all the things that we have. It is both a virtue and a positive emotion, but unlike other emotions, gratitude is outer- as opposed to inner-directed: We are grateful to someone or for something *outside* of ourselves—whether to God, people, or things. It implies our reliance on others for what they provide us and is a humbling reminder that we are not self-sufficient but connected and bound to those around us. Giving thanks is also an antidote for arrogance and entitlement, toxic attitudes that alienate us from others.

Living life in a state of deep gratitude is intentional, a long-term practice that must be cultivated with discipline, making it different from momentary gratefulness, such as thanking someone for a gift. It is living in the present moment, grateful not only for what life has given you, but also accepting the reality that you are exactly where you are supposed to be, finding the perfection in every moment. In spite of hardship, you can be thankful for even the most basic elements—that you are alive, you are breathing, and you can always find good things to celebrate. Reverend Otis J. Moss of Cleveland wrote of paying a pastoral visit to one of his congregants in the hospital who had just learned that both her legs were to be amputated. At a loss for words to comfort this woman, it was she, instead, who told him of all the wonderful things she was planning to do with her hands when she returned home, fulfilling childhood dreams of learning to sew, knit, and crochet. She then said to Reverend Moss, "I think I will bake you a cake."

If living a life of gratitude sounds like a tall order, it is. Psychologist Robert A. Emmons of the University of California, Davis, a pioneering researcher in the science of gratitude, admits his own difficulty maintaining a grace-filled worldview. Some of the impediments, he says, are that we are forgetful, take things for granted, and have high expectations. Nonetheless, he cannot envision a world in which people do not give and receive gratitude regularly. "Binding people together in relationships of reciprocity," says Emmons, "gratitude is one of the building blocks of a civil and humane society." As such, it contributes to positive relationships and civility because "we show our respect for others by recognizing their good intentions in helping us."

Although the study of the science of gratitude only began in 2000, the results of the research are indeed impressive. Grateful people experience higher levels of positive emotions such as joy, enthusiasm, love, happiness, and optimism; they are also less inclined toward jealousy and envy. Further, Emmons's studies have shown that living with gratitude increases our feelings of connectedness to others, improving our relationships and making us feel less lonely; with a deeper sense of appreciation for one another, thankful couples have stronger marriages. Grateful people feel more altruistic, loving, forgiving, spiritual, and closer to God. They are able to cope better, have deeper wellsprings of resilience, and recover more quickly from trauma and illness. Less materialistic, the grateful make fewer social comparisons with those who have more than they do. As a result, they are happier, enjoying what they have been given, not yearning for what they don't have.

Counting our blessings in life—feeling blessed—leads us to savor the moment, thus maximizing our pleasure and enjoyment. Happiness, in turn, engenders greater creativity, confidence, and willingness to help others. University of California, Riverside, psychologist Sonja Lyubomirsky, in fact, includes the practice of gratitude as one of the twelve scientifically proven strategies individuals can employ to increase their happiness by up to 40 percent.

Being on the receiving end of gratitude is also very powerful, engendering a feeling that we have contributed something useful and valuable. Neurocardiological research is beginning to show why heartfelt gratitude is so beneficial for those on the receiving end. The human heart possesses the largest rhythmic electromagnetic field of any organ in the body, more than sixty times greater than the electrical activity of the brain. Studies have shown that coherent heart rhythms, prompted by feelings of gratitude, can actually synchronize with the brain waves of another person, producing a heartfelt connection between people, and a perception of being deeply understood and appreciated.

Psychologist JoAnn Tsang found that receivers of help felt more connected and significantly more grateful when they knew that the provider had benevolent intentions toward them. In another study, Tsang showed that having and practicing gratitude also improved the lives of the caregivers of Alzheimer's patients. Simply writing about gratitude had a positive impact on their health.

> The talent for being happy is appreciating and liking what you have, instead of liking what you don't have.
>
> —WOODY ALLEN

Gratitude is a tenet of all the major religions of the world, as a way to express thanksgiving to God. In many Eastern religions, it is part of a state of enlightenment. Conversely, ingratitude, or a refusal to give thanks, is condemned universally as a moral failure. Ingratitude toward other human beings is arrogant and insulting because it precludes the "principle of reciprocity," whereby we are expected to help others who have helped us and refrain from harming anyone who has helped us. Ingratitude toward God is considered a sacrilege and blasphemy.

Yet gratitude as a practice does not come easily for people who find it difficult to depend on other people. There are also some who view themselves as victims of life's injustices. Still others focus on the scarcity of what they don't have, rather than the abundance of what they do have. As a result, there are very negative ramifications to being in a state of ingratitude. According to Emmons, "Because providing benefits and creating bonds of gratitude tie people together in society, ingratitude weakens our bonds to others." This often manifests in narcissism, self-absorption, and lack of empathy.

As we noted, intentionally practicing gratitude is not easy. It is not something you can learn overnight but must do in stages over time. You can start keeping a gratitude journal on a weekly or daily basis in which you record things for which you are grateful, breaking them down into small bits, such as an act of kindness that someone did for you. You can also make a *vow* to practice gratitude, as research has shown that taking this step stimulates people to maintain any new practice, turning it into a habit. Whatever action you take, it is okay to start small, and it is never too late to begin the practice.

❧ 26 ❧

Embody Enough

He who is greedy is ever in want.

—HORACE

To know you have enough is to be rich.

—*TAO TE CHING*

A poignant story by the late American writer Kurt Vonnegut, in tribute to his dear friend Joseph Heller, a novelist and playwright, goes as follows:

True story, Word of Honor: Joseph Heller, an important and funny writer now dead, and I were at a party given by a billionaire on Shelter Island. I said, "Joe, how does it make you feel to know that our host only yesterday may have made more money than your novel *Catch-22* has earned in its entire history?" And Joe said, "I've got something he can never have." And I said, "What on earth could that be, Joe?" And Joe said, "The knowledge that I've got enough." Not bad! Rest in peace.

The concept of *having enough* goes against the intrinsic nature of greed, that pernicious trait that, throughout history, has cost many a king his kingdom and has been a bane of lesser mortals as well. Whether the quest is for power, status, money, or the things that money can buy, greed essentially represents an excessive and insatiable desire that can never be fulfilled, a bottomless pit, a continual yearning for more. Compelling people to reach for more than what may be their proportionate share, selfish greed fosters a nearsightedness that not only blinds us to the needs of others but also undermines our sense of community, isolating and setting us apart in our self-proclaimed exclusivity.

As we pursue those aspirations, other values are often compromised; relationships with those whom we love the most can erode and suffer. Focusing on our achievements and success, we may further distance ourselves by a false belief that we are indeed masters of our own fate and beholden to none. With stunted humility, we begin to believe that we are separate from and better than other people, more worthy and entitled. Our incessant drive to chase the dream can even cause us to disconnect from ourselves, losing our grasp of who we really are deep down.

In their studies of people who are obsessed with the excessive accumulation of money, University of Exeter professors Stephen Lea and Paul Webley liken the motivation behind such acquisitiveness to a drug addiction that works on the mind, changing how we feel. We do not have to be so possessed, however, to feel the effects of money. In conjunction with various colleagues, Kathleen Vohs, a psychologist and associate professor at the University of Minnesota Carlson School of Management, has conducted studies regarding the psychological consequences and symbolic power of money. Behind Vohs's research is the premise that, in an interdependent society, social popularity and money help us get what we want and that, in most cultures, money may be a substitute for social popularity, promoting self-sufficiency.

In numerous experiments conducted in recent years in the United States, India, and China, Vohs discovered that even having visual reminders of money, such as paper play money, makes people develop greater self-sufficiency, prompting them to seek and provide less help. On one hand, groups receiving such reminders became harder workers and were willing to work longer hours in order to achieve their personal goals. However, they also became less *prosocial*, meaning that they were less willing to be helpful to others, volunteer their time, or give money to charity.

Indeed, money is a complex issue, with many of us believing that we would be happier if we only had more of it. A substantial body of research, however, points to the opposite fact: Beyond covering basic needs, having a significantly greater amount of money does not result in a significant increase in happiness. Studies of countries as well as individuals confirm the same result. Harvard social psychologist Dan Gilbert has stated, "We think money will bring lots of happiness for a long time, and actually it brings a little happiness for a short time." Moreover, current surveys of the wealthy indicate that money, within their families, often causes more problems than it solves.

So why is it that having money does not correlate to greater happiness? A number of psychologists and sociologists point to the *hedonic treadmill* or *adaptation*. As we get that bigger house and fancier car, they become a normal part of our existence. We come to expect them, so they no longer bring us the same level of happiness as they initially did. As we accumulate those material goods, we begin to compare ourselves socially to other people, stacking up our money and possessions against theirs. Making or having more money than other people becomes important. Participants in a Harvard study of faculty, staff, and students were asked to choose between earning $50,000 a year while each of the other participants made $25,000, or earning $100,000 a year while others made $200,000. Fifty-six percent preferred option one, even if it meant relinquishing an additional $50,000 in salary, because feeling richer than other people was a higher motivation for them.

While chasing money for its own sake may not promise a positive outcome, ongoing current research is looking at ways that spending money actually *can* buy happiness. Professor Elizabeth Dunn, a psychologist at the University of British Columbia, teamed up with Harvard psychology professor Michael Norton in a series of experiments that showed that *prosocial spending*—gifts for others or donations to charity—was positively correlated with a higher sense of happiness. As Dunn explains, while we may think that we "value goods over experiences, ourselves over others, things over people," research suggests what really makes us happy is giving to other people, which is why taking a friend out to dinner may provide an afterglow that buying a new dress will not.

> It is not the creation of wealth that is wrong, but the love of money for its own sake.
>
> —MARGARET THATCHER

Other researchers who are looking at how we spend money are concluding that experiential things—a vacation, an evening out on the town, a movie with friends—provide more lasting happiness than do material goods, whether they be a new car or a pair of shoes. Leaf Van Boven, associate psychology professor at the University of Colorado, and Thomas Gilovich, psychology department chair at Cornell University, in their joint study, suggest that the underlying reason for these results is that experiences with other people are more social, meeting our most basic needs as human beings. The memory of that wonderful family trip is lasting, in spite of mishaps that may have occurred at the time; accumulating material goods, on the other hand, invites more social comparisons to what other people have.

So what does it mean to embody or have *enough*? Only *you* can make that determination as you take into account values, benefits, and sacrifices. What the term *enough* implies, however, is a certain level of satisfaction and contentment with the way things are, a state of being devoid of the angst and pressure of excessive striving for something that you do not yet have.

Rather than assessing the standards of individuals, a fairer measure may be to compare countries. For three decades, social scientists and pollsters from the University of Michigan's World Values Survey, the University of Leicester, and Erasmus University Rotterdam, among others, have measured the happiness levels of countries around the world, and, consistently, Denmark tops the list. While all the surveys essentially ask, "How happy are you?" the real question is *why* the Danes are so happy. In recent years, the search for that answer has compelled news reporters from ABC's *20/20*, CBS's *60 Minutes*, the BBC, the *Washington Post*, and *The Oprah Winfrey Show* to travel to Denmark to explore possible reasons.

Researcher Kaare Christensen of the University of Southern Denmark conducted a study that concluded that his countrymen had lower expectations for their lives. He pointed out, however, that Italy and Spain had much higher expectations but were not as satisfied with their lives, which might have a lot to do with the stress and disappointment of unmet expectations.

It would be a mistake, however, to assume that the low expectation factor is the result of more modest ambitions. Instead, the Danes simply consider themselves more accepting of life's situations and realistic in their views, a state of mind that in itself alleviates stress. They also revere and model a lifestyle that balances work and personal life, along with a strong sense of family and community.

Many additional factors contribute to the Danes' happiness. Their population is largely homogenous with no great disparities of wealth. Their streets are clean and safe, and they also have faith and trust in their democratic government and in each other—two elements of trust that, according to a happiness study conducted by the University of Cambridge, appear to predominate in happier countries.

Working in a relatively stable economy, the Danes are not inclined to choose their careers based on income or status. The resulting attitude is that no one is better than anyone else. In exchange for a hefty income tax—between 50 and 70 percent—they enjoy a panoply of benefits, including health care, free university education, and child- and eldercare subsidies. As a result, the Danes have a sense of safety and security that diminishes stress and provides a significant level of contentment.

In her interviews with residents of Copenhagen, Oprah Winfrey discovered that the Danes are not enamored with possessions, preferring to live simply. As a society they share many values and priorities, including a keen sense of community and an appreciation of their strong social fabric; collectively, they exemplify what it means to *embody enough*. As one female interviewee commented, "We are very civilized, and we like to take care of each other."

Psychologist Tal Ben-Shahar, who teaches the most popular course at Harvard—"Positive Psychology: The Pursuit of Happiness"—says that Americans "want it all," which usually refers to

> We are not the sum of our possessions.
>
> —GEORGE H. W. BUSH

material things that don't make us happy. Close relationships are the number-one predictor of well-being, a common finding among many psychologists today. "Over 94 percent of college students nationwide are stressed and overwhelmed," says Ben-Shahar, a condition that starts early in life and continues throughout adulthood.

That tendency to want it all is in itself a form of greed, taxing our health and well-being as well as our relationships. Scientific evidence indicates that our drive to compete and fit in fuels a desire to accumulate even more stuff, which, in the end, won't make us happy. What that process does is make us more attached to material goods, not connect us with the people in our lives.

Although life is about balance, we each have the power as individuals to establish our values, make choices about how we want to live, and determine our own priorities and what is right for us. As you go through that process, discerning what is important, you might also want to consider what is actually *enough*.

27

Adapt Adeptly

The wise adapt themselves to circumstances,
as water moulds itself to the pitcher.
—CHINESE PROVERB

When we are no longer able to change a situation,
we are challenged to change ourselves.
—VIKTOR FRANKL

Term limits is a concept that not only applies to elective office, but is also relevant to each one of us as we live, learning daily that life is not always on our terms. Our outlook and attitude—how we adjust our sails to the winds and play the cards we are dealt—not only can shape the outcome of a situation, but also can determine our own continued viability and productivity in our lives, our families, and our communities at large. Regardless of whether changes are the result of ongoing world events or occurrences that happen to us personally, the way in which we face life and adapt—relying on our flexibility, resilience, growth, innovation, and reinvention—can make a difference in whether we thrive or decline, connect or disconnect with others. The more accepting we are of reality—what change hath wrought—as opposed to yearning for life as it once was, the more easily we will be able to adjust to life's circumstances and not be diminished by them.

World events beyond our control impact our lives in positive and negative ways. Some beckon us to learn and grow, such as new technology. Economic downturns and industrial shifts, on the other hand, result in transformations that may require us to reinvent ourselves completely, as some jobs fade while other opportunities open up. Many of these events are so sweeping and cataclysmic that they potentially can influence the evolution of our society and civilization. Think the Internet. Think 9/11. Think the Great Recession that commenced in 2008. Our awareness and desire to stay current or not—"tuning in" by knowing and getting involved, or "tuning out" by ignoring and resisting—may ultimately determine our success in keeping up with life rather than being defeated by it and having it pass us by.

Change in the world is inevitable and occurring at an exponential rate. For example, a 2008 presentation prepared by researchers for the top executives of Sony purports that China will soon be the number-one English-speaking country in the world. Many of today's jobs didn't exist ten years ago, and present-day learners will have somewhere between ten and fourteen jobs by the time they are thirty-eight. While it took thirty-eight years for radio to reach an audience of fifty million, it took the Internet only four and Facebook two.

How we deal with change affects our interpersonal relationships as well. In times of crisis, we may withdraw, pushing away those who love us and wish to help us through our difficulties. Frustrated, angry, or depressed, we may blame others for our circumstances, pointing the finger at friends, coworkers, or even entire groups of people whom we blame for our misfortune. Or, we may connect and grow closer to one another, as friends and family, by reaching out and offering support and sustenance to those in need, as well as by accepting the same when the circumstances are reversed. We may learn to embrace changes positively— such as new technologies—without losing each other along the way, by making sure that such technology does not substitute for face-to-face interactions that bind us together as a community. While there are many things in this world that are beyond our control, the way we choose to interact with and treat one another is within our reach.

> Experience is not what happens to you; it's how you interpret what happens to you.
>
> —ALDOUS HUXLEY

Personal misfortune and adversity often require a total readjustment if we are to survive, emotionally as well as physically. Accidents, death, divorce, health concerns, the loss of a job, or acts of nature may cause an upheaval that knocks us down in such a way that we need a different toolkit to meet the challenge and ultimately rebound. In those circumstances, positivity plays a determining factor in our resilience, says University of North Carolina psychology professor Barbara Fredrickson, because it may be the lifeline that keeps us from spiraling downward into negative emotion and even clinical depression. A positive attitude might be our best tool in a crisis.

Citing numerous research studies, Fredrickson refers to the "undo-effect" of positive emotions, or the way that the positive flushes out the negative. It is simply impossible to experience both at the same time. For instance, we cannot be relaxed and tense simultaneously. Her conclusion is that resilient people are emotionally nimble as well as highly attuned to life's ever-changing circumstances. They don't waste energy worrying about the future; instead, they cope with whatever happens. In addition, they neither overgeneralize nor overreact. According to Fredrickson, "The openness that comes with positivity is what enables them to see the big picture, appreciate the now, and find the good within the bad. Openness dissolves negativity and enables people to make a comeback."

While none of us has a road map in life, staying current on what is happening in the world—locally and globally—can help us plot our options and direction so that we stay on top of our game in an evolving civilization. Whether we are facing joyous or trying times, our strength and vitality come from our ability to draw on our resources—internal and external—and adapt adeptly, so that we remain connected to others and tuned in, as contributing members of society.

28

Practice Patience

Patience is the ability to idle your motor when
you feel like stripping your gears.
—BARBARA JOHNSON

I am extraordinarily patient,
provided I get my own way in the end.
—MARGARET THATCHER

This chapter is purposely titled "Practice Patience," in part because it
serves as a reminder to myself that this is one area of my life that could
benefit from more significant attention. Because it is a particularly short
suit of mine, my family might even joke that my writing about the topic is
akin to the pot calling the kettle black. Undoubtedly, impatience is a powerful negative energy running through the population today, a tense current that is inextricably linked to stress and our hurried lifestyles. As a
result, it is a major contributing factor to our vastly rude culture.

One of the seven heavenly virtues in Catholic catechism, patience is considered a core spiritual practice and an important theme in many world
religions. Numerous references to the merits of patience can be found
throughout the Bible. In Judaism, the Talmud lauds patience as an important attribute, and the Torah mentions patience in several of its proverbs.
Muslims believe that they can grow closer to Allah by practicing patience,
particularly through suffering, and that Allah will be with them through
that suffering.

In the larger realm of religion, patience is equated with perseverance and
endurance without complaint, irritation, anger, or annoyance. It is also

related to tolerance and steadfastness in the face of hardship, difficulty, and suffering as well as the ability to delay gratification. Hence, patience is spiritually embraced as one of the most highly touted virtues in life.

Whether or not you take this longer and deeper spiritual view of patience, having the ability to be patient makes life far easier, more enjoyable, and less stressful and combative. When you are patient, you accept life as it is, without frenzy, struggle, or attempting to change it to suit your terms. That acceptance of the here and now allows you to more fluidly "go with the flow"—swimming with the current, rather than against the stream. That acceptance gives us an inner peace.

Living life based on the clock is a root cause of our impatience. On a daily basis, clocks rule our agendas, as we rush from here to there—late, late, late—never with enough time to complete our tasks or finish our work because we've packed too much into too short a time. In a larger sense, time is the yardstick by which we measure our expectations—becoming an executive vice president by age twenty-five, or retiring by forty.

Deadlines are sometimes arbitrarily set—in stone—for our goals and accomplishments. Time can be a tyrannical master, and our impatience the lash that drives us forward against the clock. Hence, as Russian writer Leo Tolstoy wrote, "The two most powerful warriors are patience and time."

> A hot-tempered man stirs up dissension, but a patient man calms a quarrel.
>
> —PROVERBS 15:18 (NEW INTERNATIONAL VERSION)

When those deadlines are unmet, we often allow our impatience to rule our behavior. That's where "Me first" and "I'll get mine" kick in and take over, and we turn ugly. We signal that our agendas are more important than anyone else's as we roll our eyes and groan while standing in a slow-moving line or bark at others for delaying us. In our impatience and haste, we make mistakes, make poor decisions, cause accidents, and fracture relationships.

When patience is short, so are our tempers with our spouses and children. We become irritated with coworkers whose productivity does not measure up to our standards. Our impatience impedes progress in a stalled negotiation as our negativity swells, blinding us to possibilities. Displeased, we are quick to throw up our hands, absolve ourselves of responsibility, and blame the other person, which solves nothing. We judge people as fools, whom we don't suffer gladly.

In a culture where everything is increasingly fast, our impatience fuels our entitlement for immediate gratification. We want what we want, and we want it *now*. What we often fail to realize is that some things just take time to play out. As one unknown author wrote, "Patience is waiting. Not passively waiting. That is laziness. But to keep going when the going is hard and slow—that is patience."

Impatience prevents us from being fully present, depriving us of the richness of life. By contrast, patience gives us space to just *be*. As a result, patience is not just soothing but also healing, as we discover just how good those roses smell. Patience helps us manage our expectations—both of ourselves and of others. By becoming aware of our impatience and what triggers it, we are better able to get a handle on it and maintain self-restraint and control. Slowly, calmly, softly. Patience not only teaches us lessons, but it also provides a space in which to learn them.

29

Drive Gently on the Road

It takes 8,460 bolts to assemble an automobile,
and one nut to scatter it all over the road.

—ANONYMOUS

There's nothing quite like driving a car to bring out the worst in us, and no place where our collective rudeness and competitive one-upmanship is more blatantly visible than on the roadway. Something happens to us when faced with the daily challenges behind the wheel of an automobile; even souls who are ordinarily rational and calm are apt to morph into altered states when the trespasses of fellow motorists get them going. With equanimity shattered, we're ready for combat—against foe and friend alike.

To begin, let's consider the importance of cars in our lives. We take deep pride in owning them, so that they become, in a certain sense, extensions of ourselves. Although some people acquire particular vehicles as status symbols, cars allow us to be mobile, giving us a sense of reach and power: They often make us appear and act "bigger" than we are. And because they also provide a shelter on wheels, they become a domain of sorts, a home away from home, endowing us with a certain mobile territory and personal space, which we ferociously protect with offensive and defensive maneuvering. Thus, we go about claiming "what is ours"—what we feel entitled to.

Unfortunately, cars also grant us anonymity, which shields our identity as perpetrators of unspeakable acts of rudeness, carelessness, and revenge. And when we think we can get away with something, we often take that license. At a four-way intersection, we come to a rolling stop and jump ahead of others before they take their deserved turns. Or, without a speck of generosity, we look the other way when another driver is begging to merge in front of us. Much more dangerously, we dart in and out of traffic at high speeds, leaving no more than a hairbreadth between vehicles, often squeezing a less assertive driver out of a lane. Or we ride the bumper of the car in front of us, bearing down with all our might until the slowpoke gets out of our way. If the police aren't in sight, we might take a chance and run through a red light or a pedestrian crossing.

Does any of this behavior sound familiar? Is this ever you? Sadly, most of us are guilty of some of these acts, at least on occasion. *Everybody* seems to be in a hurry, with too much to do in too little time. And when we are delayed, our temperature rises from a slow simmer to a roiling boil.

What we do to ourselves in this heightened state of anxiety is bad enough. What we often fail to consider is how our bad behavior makes others feel angry and abused, creating a ripple effect whereby they abuse others. The result is often aggression, which can escalate into violence that not only endangers but also can kill people.

> The best car safety device is a rear-view mirror with a cop in it.
>
> —DUDLEY MOORE

Speaking of that outcome, two thousand to three thousand deaths occur on the roads every year due to the distractions of our incessant multitasking while driving, and more than a hundred times that many are injured. A number of studies have shown that using a cell phone while driving can be at least as dangerous as having a blood alcohol level over the legal limit; texting can slow a driver's reaction time by 35 percent. Researchers from the University of Utah reported that only 2.5 percent of the population is capable of "supertasking" without impairment; on average, it took participants 20 percent longer to brake when talking on a cell phone.

While there are laws in only a few states banning the use of handheld cell phones, enforcement by authorities remains an issue. Each and every time any of us picks up a cell phone while driving a vehicle we endanger our own lives as well as those around us. Unfortunately, a 2010 report from the Pew Internet and American Life Project indicated that 27 percent of drivers admitted to texting while driving.

So what does it take to make us stop? Are we capable of restraining our "driving ambition" to be king of the road, or must we destroy a life in order to learn a lesson?

Our safety and that of others often depends on our self-restraint and control. When another driver has merely one-upped us by cutting us off or by taking our turn at an intersection, we need to get a grip and slough off the incident, rather than allowing it to ruin our day. For our own sakes, the AAA Foundation for Traffic Safety recommends not making eye contact with an aggressive driver because staring can turn the encounter into a duel. They further advise not hogging the passing lane—even if you're going the speed limit—because you can incite the anger of fellow drivers.

Driving on the road is certainly an arena to practice kindness and generosity, creating innumerable positive ripples that make everyone's day better. So next time, invite a fellow driver to merge in front of you, or hang back so that you're not bearing down on someone else's bumper. Remember—we're all traveling the same road together!

30

Pick Your
Battles Wisely

If you treat every situation as a life and death matter,
you'll die a lot of times.

—DEAN SMITH

There is an old aphorism: "It isn't the mountains ahead that wear you out, it's the grain of sand in your shoe." Although those grains may amount to little more than petty grievances, over time they not only irritate but can also fray the edges of our relationships. If we bury our annoyance, our resentment may build so that we blow a fuse, overreact, and have a meltdown. By the same token, it's not healthy to live in an emotional state in which *everything* is high drama, so that you're constantly hacking away at other people, whether it's your spouse, your children, your friends, or your colleagues. That sort of behavior is disruptive and tiresome for everyone concerned.

So what do you do? Pick your battles wisely. Sometimes this tactic is a process, requiring both insight and foresight in order to decide what is really important and what is not. It's also helpful to bear in mind that you're probably not going to "win" every skirmish; you don't want to pick fights all the time. Keep in mind that what is important to me might not be so important to you and vice versa.

Often it is better simply not to "sweat the small stuff" and to let some things roll off your back, since they aren't worth upsetting yourself and ruining your day. Those minor irritations—a shopper who swoops in and grabs the last can of peas just as you were about to, or your spouse forgetting to pick up your suit at the dry cleaner—might be things that aren't worth the fuss. However, a friend who chooses not to speak to you for days, or a neighbor whose dog finds your yard a choice dumping ground, might well be the sorts of issues that grab your attention.

While I have no magic prescription for which issues a person should take on, I generally try to ignore those onetime situations with people I don't know or probably will not see again ... but not always. Not long ago, in a grocery store, I discovered that my cart had suddenly gone missing while I was choosing produce items. Not wanting to repeat the shopping I had already done, I spent a full ten minutes looking for my cart, figuring that another customer had taken it by mistake. Upon locating it, I expected to have a little laugh with the well-intentioned "cart thief." To my surprise, I was confronted with a shopper who matter-of-factly said that, since she had by now accumulated more items than I previously had, it was up to me to get another cart. Flabbergasted and, for once, at a total loss for words at this lady's chutzpah, I also realized that this was a nonnegotiable stance on her part. Still dumbfounded, I retrieved another cart and transferred my items into it.

> If you want to test your memory, try to recall what you were worrying about one year ago today.
>
> —E. JOSEPH COSSMAN

Continuing to shop, I fumed, obsessing over this lady's act. This was one time that I couldn't let the issue go. Surmising that she might still be in the store, I decided to find her and let her know how she had mishandled the situation. With her back turned to me, I tapped her shoulder. When she spun around, before I could even open my mouth, she called out, "Truce! I'm sorry!" At that point, I let the matter drop, holding back any recriminating response. Sometimes, you just have to let it go. The trick is to know when.

31

Remember What Your Mother Taught You

Good manners:
The noise you don't make when eating your soup.
—BENNETT CERF

I frequently ask the attendees in my seminars to define what etiquette means to them. Often, college students describe it as "hoity-toity behavior," grandmother's tea party, or fancy dinners with silver and crystal. One young woman went so far as to say that it is behavior relevant only to upper and upper-middle classes. Unfortunately, those are common misperceptions that have no bearing on what etiquette is about: rules that make social interactions and events flow more smoothly.

While the rules are often referred to as "social graces," they apply to almost every arena in our daily lives. You can't play a game of golf without knowing golf etiquette. Every tennis player knows that you don't retrieve your ball on the adjacent court while the other game is in play. There is an accepted theater decorum in which you neither talk nor disturb others once the movie or play has begun. At the symphony, you don't applaud between movements. In fitness centers, you neither hog the machines nor take up more than your share of "mat space" in a yoga class. There is expected behavior in a classroom or lecture, as well as procedural etiquette in a courtroom, in a meeting, for elections, while driving, and many rituals of life, including weddings and funerals. In short, the rules of etiquette provide structure and order in almost every aspect of our lives, and they serve as behavioral guidelines and norms to help prevent us from offending others.

Your knowledge and practice of these rules can impact how fluidly you interact with people—or not—and how you are perceived by others. The manner in which you present yourself can impact whether you are hired for a job or your success in rising on a career ladder. Your good behavior reflects your sensitivity to others as well as a particular environment. Manners matter.

Sadly, we often find ourselves surrounded by noticeably crude people, as their coarse and repelling behavior makes them stand out above the crowd. For instance, if you've ever been in the company of one who, mouth agape, chomps her meal, you'll likely decline the rest of yours, particularly if she simultaneously slurps and smacks her lips, spraying food across the table as she talks—a sure-fire appetite suppressant. Blowing one's nose into a napkin will produce much the same effect on fellow tablemates, as will scratching your head or playing with your hair. It is also impolite to stick your fork into another person's food without asking, to take a sample bite. These are not uncommon aberrations, which many find nauseating.

Boorish behavior is by no means confined to the table. Sometimes the discourtesy of others can literally make you sick; for example, when someone unconscionably sneezes on you or coughs without covering his mouth. This goes beyond mere inconsideration, particularly when illnesses such as flu viruses threaten to become pandemic.

Talking or laughing too loudly is disconcerting when others around you are conversing. We're all familiar with the stereotype of the overly jolly bigmouth who slaps your back and pumps your arm up and down so forcefully that you fear its dislocation. However, it is worse not to notice or greet people at all.

> Manners are very communicable: men catch them from each other.
>
> —RALPH WALDO EMERSON

Except in certain cultures, the sound of belching and burping adults is not music to anyone's ears, nor is the expulsion of gas an occasion for high-fives. While body noises and potty humor are sources of great amusement among the kindergarten set, anyone continuing that amusement beyond a certain age is in need of serious maturation.

Of course, not every repugnant offense is noisy. Poor personal hygiene and body odor are silent assaults, guaranteed to clear bystanders within a multifoot radius. Shaking hands with someone who has dirty fingernails can be so off-putting that some avoid contact altogether. And while a physical space may not need to pass a white-glove inspection, cleanliness indeed may be related to "godliness," as the results of a study titled "The Smell of Virtue" indicate. The coauthors, professors of management at Brigham Young University, the University of Toronto, and Northwestern University, concluded that "people are unconsciously fairer and more generous when they are in clean-smelling environments."

There's no single word that encompasses the full range of uncouth behavior, although Mother may have mentioned slovenly, slothful, sloppy, or a slob, particularly when taking stock of your disheveled appearance. She may have used *pigsty* when describing your room or *piggy* in reference to your manners. Regrettably, there are many adults who give pigs a bad name as they go for the biggest piece of pie or grab the last cookie. And nothing, it seems, inspires gluttony like an all-you-can-eat buffet, to which some react as though it were a last call for food on earth. With plates piled high, they alternately stampede and gorge themselves, from buffet table to dining table—and back again.

There are countless more examples of distasteful behaviors that are offensive and disgusting to other people—behaviors that may cause you to lose respect or isolate you from people you might want as friends. Mother may have said that polish is not just for shoes, and with good reason. As the late actress Lillian Gish once noted, "You can get through life with bad manners, but it's easier with good manners." A little refinement and smoothing out your rough edges goes a long way toward easing your way in the world and getting along with other people. Those polished interpersonal skills are the social grease that doesn't soil, but instead helps you to connect.

32

Teach Your Children Well

The hardest job facing kids is learning good
manners without seeing any.
—FRED ASTAIRE

If you must hold yourself up to your children
as an object lesson, hold yourself up as a warning,
not an example.
—GEORGE BERNARD SHAW

The toys that we buy our children often have a dual purpose. Building blocks, for example, are intended both to be fun and to help develop fine motor skills. Books build vocabulary, and the stories often relate life lessons.

Making eye contact, smiling, and waving "bye bye" are unwitting introductory forms of appropriate social interactions from which babies learn how to communicate. As they mature, we teach them basic manners and social skills that engender consideration, age-appropriate behavior, and the ability to cooperate and get along with others.

By age two, children should be taught that hitting and biting are inappropriate, since those behaviors are overtly harmful to others. In school, they begin to learn that there are other disruptive behaviors that both impact the order of the classroom and impair the learning of others. Manners are about our consideration for others, which fosters more harmonious relationships—important life lessons that require due diligence on the part of parents in teaching them.

Sadly, many child development experts, including pediatricians and psychologists, are observing a shift away from teaching these social codes, with children often not receiving the same guidance from parents as they did a couple of generations ago. Many child development professionals are witnessing parents who frequently are unable to set limits and say no to their kids, who in turn become increasingly rude and demanding as they grow. Harvard-trained pediatrician Dr. Perri Klass wrote in the *New York Times* that, while she does not record "rude" or "polite" in a patient's chart, she does make a judgment along those lines, as do other pediatricians. And when she sees young patients in her office who seemingly have no manners, she considers not only what may be happening in a child's life—at home or at school—but also the possibility of a neurodevelopmental problem.

Experts almost universally agree on the importance of teaching manners, beginning at an early age, as part of a child's socialization process. Dr. Barbara Howard, an assistant professor of pediatrics at the Johns Hopkins University School of Medicine and an expert on behavior and development, is quoted as saying, "Social skills are necessary for school success; they affect how you do on the playground, in the classroom, in the workplace."

Etiquette professionals often lament that teaching manners began to take a dive in the late 1960s and 1970s as the baby boomer generation, with their countercultural values, came of age. Merging into the workforce, however, boomers largely fell back into more traditional roles, resurrecting the manners with which they were raised; unfortunately, they didn't necessarily pass them along to their offspring.

Next came generation X, the "latchkey kids," so-called because of the increasing number of households with two working parents as well as split families. With 40 percent of gen Xers left home alone, they are considered by many researchers to have been among the *least* nurtured in American history. Many went on to become parents of generation Y, often referred to as the *most* indulged children in history.

It has been said that the overly permissive parents of gen Y, blamed for coddling and hovering, were so invested in their children's feelings and the importance of self-esteem that they did not stress that anyone else's feelings mattered. Thus, strict adherence to a structure of codified rules diminished, as did the children's respect and consideration for other people.

In their zeal to provide their children with every competitive advantage, parents who clamored for their children to play Mozart by age three too often left social skills out of the educational equation. (A ten-year study published in 2008 by the University of Illinois, however, reported that social skills are a more accurate indicator of a person's future work success than test scores. Had this study come out twenty years ago, it is possible that many of these parents, eager to ensure their children's favorable outcome as adults, may have emphasized an altogether different set of values in raising their children.)

Another reason for the laxity in teaching manners today may be that the parents themselves do not know how to behave appropriately because no one ever taught them. Further, many parents holding down two jobs are already so stressed with work and dealing with their kids' schedules that there is no time even to eat dinner together, much less teach manners. As a result, they want the time that they do spend together to be stress-free with as few conflicts as possible.

> Parents who are afraid to put their foot down usually have children who step on their toes.
>
> —CHINESE PROVERB

Obviously, these observations do not pertain to every family. More often than not, however, children mirror the behavior that they see—positive and negative—and when they observe grown-ups who are disrespectful, rude, and nasty when they don't get their way, the children have little reason to act otherwise. "Do as I say, not as I do" has never been a convincing lesson.

For instance, a survey of 23,000 adults in twenty-two countries found that more than 35 percent of adults worldwide have witnessed a parent become physically or verbally abusive toward a coach or another official at a children's sporting event. The survey, jointly conducted by Reuters and the market research company Ipsos, reported that America topped the list, with 60 percent of respondents having witnessed such a spectacle, followed by India, with 59 percent. Further, the adults most likely to have witnessed such incidents were in higher income brackets and had attained higher levels of education. This does not present a pretty picture of parents as role models.

There are also other societal influences. Dr. Susan Linn, professor of psychiatry at Harvard Medical School and director of the Campaign for a

Commercial-Free Childhood, points to the stories and toys from which children also learn, as well as a commercial culture that glamorizes rudeness and violence. Others agree. The media showcases these negative behaviors, making them appear so ordinary that they become the norm. Further, toys and video games where kids engage in aggressive virtual behavior are also to blame.

Little people will carry forth the legacy that we pass on. Unless we want an increasingly chaotic society, we have to be willing to make an investment in teaching our kids age-appropriate behavior, manners, and respect for others. We must provide boundaries and guidelines for being kind and compassionate and treating people well. Manners and good behavior are all about caring for others and being sensitive to their feelings. They are about being compassionate and learning to get along in society at every age of life. Above all, they require us to model the same behavior that we expect of our children.

33

Bring Back the Magic

Silent gratitude isn't much use to anyone.
—G. B. STERN

It is a continual source of amazement to me that *please*, *thank you*, and *excuse me* so often elude the lips of so many adults. These are the first "magic" words that we teach our children if they are to know anything at all about basic courtesy, laying the foundation for other rules of polite interaction that help us fluidly engage others throughout life.

Through simple dialogue we begin the lesson:

JOHNNY: I want a cookie.
MOMMY: What do you say?
JOHNNY: *Please*, may I have a cookie?
MOMMY: Good. Now what do you say?
JOHNNY: I forgot.
MOMMY: *Excuse me*, Johnny, but you know better.
JOHNNY: *Thank you* for the cookie.

These simple words teach a child appreciation not simply for the cookie but also for the person giving him the cookie. By expressing gratitude, he is showing an understanding of how humanity functions respectfully.

If this lesson works so well to get what we want in childhood, why do we find it any less useful when we grow up? I don't mean to imply that manners are manipulative tools to garner what we want, although children learn early on that they are more likely to get that cookie by using the magic words and asking nicely.

When an adult fails to say *please* or *thank you* in anticipation of or in response to a thoughtful gesture or random act of kindness, or *excuse me*

when disturbing others, it is not only downright rude but also an indica-
tion of arrogance and entitlement. These are not difficult words, and they
make all the difference when they are part of an exchange, as shown in the
following scenario:

> Mr. Smith is about to approach an ATM and notices that Mr.
> Jones, rushed and agitated, is right behind him. Generously, Mr.
> Smith offers to let Mr. Jones go first.
>
> Mr. Jones fails to acknowledge Mr. Smith or his extended gen-
> erosity. Making no eye contact, he focuses his attention on the
> keypad of the ATM.
>
> Incredulous at the slight, Mr. Smith asks himself silently, "What
> does this guy think I am—a piece of cellophane?" Angry that his
> kind gesture went unappreciated, Mr. Smith broods the rest of the
> afternoon, wondering, "What's wrong with people?" As he finishes
> his own transaction, he breezes through the door, allowing it to
> slam in the face of a mother with a stroller in tow.
>
> Mrs. Blake, wrestling with her stroller, asks herself, "What's
> wrong with people? Can't they even take two seconds to hold a
> door?" By the time she enters the bank, she is livid, causing her
> to bark at the bank teller, Mr. Hall, who now laments, "Why are
> there so many rude people in the world?" Afterward, Mr. Hall
> snaps at the next customer in line. And so on....

What may sound like an insignificant occurrence is more consequential than may first
appear. In failing to acknowledge an act of generosity with simple gratitude, we are telling
people not only that we take them for granted
but also that they mean nothing to us. Our disregard hurts people's feelings, who then may go
on to hurt others. Unfortunately, it is a phenomenon that is so frequent and widespread, it
has become symptomatic of a society where we
neither care nor show concern; worse, *we don't
even notice.*

Feeling gratitude
and not expressing it
is like wrapping a
present and not
giving it.

—WILLIAM ARTHUR WARD

There are times when it isn't possible to thank someone verbally, which is where "doing the wave" is useful. For instance, when someone allows you to merge ahead in traffic, acknowledge the kindness by waving—even a nod will do!

So these basic terms—*please*, *thank you*, and *excuse me*—are no small words. They reflect a recipient's humility, gratitude, graciousness, and caring, nullifying entitlement. The giver, in turn, feels that both he and his gesture are appreciated. The result is an exchange of two kind acts. These are magic words regardless of your age; unfortunately, their inherent power is sometimes more noticeable when they are not used than when they are. It is amazing, nevertheless, how effective they can be, especially when you really want that cookie.

34

Mind Your Cybermanners

I hear YouTube, Twitter, and Facebook are merging
to form a supersocial media site—YouTwitFace.

—CONAN O'BRIEN

The Internet, which has become a nearly indispensable global communications tool in only a few short years, has afforded many positive benefits, far outweighing its drawbacks. Whatever your personal view, it is fair to say that the Internet, in all its forms, has altered the way that most of us communicate interpersonally.

In July 2010, the Pew Research Center issued a report, "The Internet and the Future of Social Relations," based on 895 respondents, 371 of whom were technology experts. Asked to project, in 2020, whether the Internet will have produced a mostly positive or negative effect on the larger picture of their social relationships, 85 percent foresaw the Internet as a positive influence.

Less face-to-face time, however, was one mentioned downside, with the residual effect of more superficial relationships and a greater tendency toward isolation. Privacy is all but eliminated, as a form of global voyeurism opens the door to public scrutiny. The Internet is also seen as engendering intolerance, according to the report. That intolerance is visible in instant messaging and smear campaigns that can range from direct one-on-one bullying to the widespread distribution of lies and half-truths. When anonymity is a factor, the invisible writer can blaspheme and destroy reputations or spew vulgarities and ugly comments without restraint, which is not unlike any other bad behavior whereby offenders think they can "get away with it" because they neither know nor see the targets of their actions.

Lack of civility is actually driving some people *away* from certain forms of Internet use. In June 2010, the global public relations firm Weber Shandwick released a poll, conducted in conjunction with Powell Tate and KRC Research, of one thousand Americans who were asked how civility affected their views on social networking, politics, media, and buying behaviors. Thirty-four percent reported that they were "tuning out" of online sites, with almost 40 percent of those doing so largely due to incivility. Asked to rate the civility of eighteen different areas of daily life, 51 percent found blogs to be the most uncivil, followed by social networking sites (43 percent), and Twitter (35 percent). Incivility on blogs was attributed largely to anonymous posts; by comparison, respondents perceived social networks as more personal, attracting people with shared interests and providing accountability in terms of who is speaking. However, the poll revealed defections from those sites as well, due to uncivil behavior or comments.

> Indecency, vulgarity, obscenity—these are strictly confined to man; he invented them. Among the higher animals, there is no trace of them.
>
> —MARK TWAIN

All cybercommunication tools—e-mail, social media networks, Twitter, blogs, or YouTube—have one thing in common, and that is *instant transmission* once the SEND button is pressed. The message, whatever its content, then flies, never to be recovered, and is modified only when a subsequent message is transmitted. It is the same as writing in ink; it cannot be erased. While the advantage of these forms of communication is speed, so is it a disadvantage. Haste, particularly when fueled by negative emotion, prompts us to make errors in facts and judgment, diminishes our ability to see the big picture, and often leads to a misguided tone—intended or otherwise. The Internet abbreviates our time, and thus ability, to be thoughtful. In the words of the late French writer Alphonse de Lamartine, "Good manners require space and time."

It is not possible to have a discussion about cybermanners without mentioning cell phones and other electronic handheld devices. While we each have our own gripes and concerns, an Intel survey indicated that nine out of ten respondents had pet peeves regarding mobile-device usage, 72 percent of whom pointed to texting while driving as their chief complaint. In addition:

- Fifty-six percent were annoyed by breaches of mobile etiquette rules in cafes and restaurants.

- Forty-seven percent were bothered by the use of cell phones in theaters and concert arenas.

- Other respondents complained about the use of mobile devices in, of all places, public bathrooms; the sound of conversations or typing was also considered annoying at a worship service, at a funeral, and in a doctor's office.

Regardless of whether you know the person with whom you are communicating or about whom you are commenting, the unspoken guidelines for cyberspace conversation are no different than for face-to-face interactions. Treating people in the same manner as you would like to be treated—with respect, dignity, and kindness—is no different within a cybercommunity than it is in a physical space. The same polite behavior applies, whether it is your choice of words, managing your emotions, or showing respect for the personal boundaries of others.

Additionally, be prudent in your posts on social network sites, because messages and pictures that reveal compromised behavior are better left undisclosed. Employers commonly search Facebook pages for information that can tell them something about the real you, so those posts can come back to bite. Don't spread rumors, gossip, or vitriol about others for the whole social network to see. Likewise, don't spread untruths or lie about who you are; many a person on Internet dating sites has been surprised to discover that the prospective date she meets in person bears little resemblance to the identity projected online.

Be as cautious about how you behave as a social cyberbutterfly as you are in person. The best advice is to be respectful, be discreet, and be nice!

35

Time It Right

Unfaithfulness in the keeping of an appointment
is an act of clear dishonesty. You may as well
borrow a person's money as his time.
—HORACE MANN

I've been on a calendar,
but I've never been on time.
—MARILYN MONROE

G. K. Chesterton, a British gentleman and one of the most prodigious writers of the twentieth century, was a man so ebullient, so in awe and appreciative of life, and so engaged in the excitement of the present moment, that his present-mindedness often led him to be quite absent-minded. As Robert A. Emmons endearingly wrote of him, Chesterton did most of his writing in a train station, because he was always apt to miss the train he was supposed to catch. Once, having a glass of wine with a relative, he suddenly remembered that he was shortly due to be delivering a lecture in another town. Yet another time, he telegraphed his wife to beseechingly inquire, "Where ought I be?"

Although his tardiness was unintentional, we don't know how those around the otherwise charming Chesterton reacted. Given our hectic schedules today, however, there are few things as inconsiderate as keeping people waiting. Obviously, we overlook those occasional times when someone is detained due to circumstances beyond her control, as we ourselves have been in the same position. However, it is the habitual offender, the one who must be told to arrive an hour early just so he shows up at the same time as other guests, who not only tries our patience but also tests the strength of our relationships.

Quite simply, there's no excuse for chronic lateness. If, for instance, you are late because you are a perpetually poor planner, other areas of your life besides relationships will suffer, such as deadlines at work. But to consistently inconvenience other people by making them wait is negligent and disrespectful. Chronic lateness conveys that either you do not care about another person's time (as well as the person) or your own time is more valuable. Either way, it signals arrogance.

Some people can be forgiven for running behind because of the nature of their jobs. (President Clinton was constantly encouraged by his schedulers to "move along" because, like Chesterton, he would get so immersed in conversation that groups of people were kept waiting at subsequent stops. His handlers jokingly referred to their boss's clock as "Clinton time.")

We might expect to wait for hours in a hospital emergency room, or for a few minutes in a doctor's office. However, the medical office that consistently overbooks an appointment schedule, keeping patients waiting for hours on end, is clearly inconsiderate. One of our family specialists was notorious for this practice. One day when, yet again, I was kept waiting two hours, I voiced my annoyance to the nurse, who urged me to confront the doctor. When he finally came in, I jokingly suggested that he pass out those buzzing electronic gadgets that large restaurants use, with flashing lights that illuminate when your table is ready. That would enable me and other patients to, say, run an errand in the neighborhood rather than sit for hours waiting. Ever since, I've not waited for more than fifteen minutes.

People count up the faults of those who keep them waiting.

—FRENCH PROVERB

Failing to show up without advance notice is even worse than making someone wait. Some professional establishments are beginning to charge for such indiscretions. Time lost waiting for a client who never shows is lost revenue that can never be replaced, but that's not all. Economics—the study of how people deal with scarcity—enumerates *time* as one of the five limited resources, along with labor, human ingenuity, land, and capital. For instance, you may want to run ten errands, but only have time to run two. Time is a resource that cannot be replaced.

Punctuality is a measure of your reliability; it is your commitment to do what you say you're going to do, whether it's keeping an appointment or meeting deadlines. Following through says that you respect the other person as well as the reason for spending that time together. To do otherwise is not just inconsiderate, it is hubris. Remember that other people are busy, just as you are.

~~ 36 ~~

Delight Your Host,
Please Your Guest

If it were not for guests, all houses would be graves.
—KAHLIL GIBRAN

In a day and age when there are so many serious global issues and problems to be solved, it may seem that the act of entertaining or attending organized social gatherings is trivial. Rest assured that it is not. A more appropriate perception would be to recognize the inherent intent and value of these occasions as opportunities to come together, celebrate, and connect interpersonally, as families, friends, associates, and new acquaintances. It is often how business "gets done," away from the office, and how relationships are forged. The fact that we lead such busy lives makes these moments even more extraordinary, particularly when our limited time constrains our ability to be social.

Fortunately, I grew up in a family that enjoyed extending warm and genuine hospitality to family and friends alike who sometimes just appeared—invited or not—and they were never turned away. Thus, I experienced early on the value of gathering and coming to the table.

Today, with our limited time, entertaining others has to be carefully slotted into our busy schedules. As a result, having an event often requires greater planning than before. One crucial element that makes any gathering flow more smoothly is consideration—both the guest's toward the host and vice versa.

The first rule of being a guest is to let your host know that you plan to be one, or not. Whether the invitation is to "come for coffee" or to a reception for five hundred, a host simply has to know whether a guest plans to show up or not, which is why an RSVP is so essential. The abbreviation, which stands for the French phrase *réspondez s'il vous plaît* (respond if you please), is a request from the host asking whether you plan to attend. Of course, you don't have to respond in French; what is important is that you do reply, and in a timely manner.

Imagine that you are planning a party and have invited fifty people. Two days before the party, you have received only six responses. Concerned, you either e-mail or leave voice-mail messages, but even this inconvenient effort on your part only produces a few definite replies. Do you buy expensive food and drink and risk throwing much of it away, or do you buy half that amount, and end up with skimpy offerings to an unexpected overflow? If the event is a wedding reception with a sit-down dinner, the expense is, decidedly, a significant factor, as are many variables, including cost per person, the seating arrangements, the size of the facility, and other relevant factors. If you have recently received any such invitation, please bear in mind this obligation as a guest and respond; otherwise, you are putting your host in an impossible position.

It's also important for a guest to be on time. If you are late, apologize, or if you know that you're going to be late, call ahead. I once hosted a dinner party at which one guest breezily arrived ninety minutes late without apology or explanation. Having extended the cocktail hour twice as long as planned, I immediately ushered everyone to the table. Before even sitting down, oblivious to the fact that she had already tortured my timetable, as well as the food that had been warming too long on the stove, that same guest passed around photos that she insisted everyone must view that very minute. She had absolutely no concept of the disrespect and inconsideration she had shown her hosts and the other guests.

A gracious guest can also bring a small but carefully chosen gift for the host—a bottle of wine, flowers, a book—as a token of gratitude. Don't, for example, bring liquor to a Muslim home or a box of chocolates to a diabetic. Another sign of respect is to dress appropriately; if in doubt, ask the host in advance. If the occasion is informal, you can offer to help before, during, or after the meal or party. However, some hosts enjoy having guests do hands-on preparations while others do not. One of my dear friends, when asked whether she needed help in the kitchen, would invariably answer, "Yes, please don't!"

Above all, one of your most important contributions as a guest is to participate fully in the event, because it's excruciating for any host to have a dinner or a party where no one interacts. Think of such events as opportunities to get to know other people and for them to know you. We have so little time these days to entertain or be entertained that it behooves us to savor those moments so that we connect, not disconnect, with others.

If you are staying in someone's home overnight or for several days, be tidy, be helpful, and look after yourself, rather than depending on a host to entertain you twenty-four hours a day. Offer to do chores, make meals, or run errands, and don't overstay your welcome. Most important, write a note of thanks afterward.

The counterpoint to being a good guest is being a genuinely welcoming host. Just as guests have obligations, so do hosts, as you are offering a gift of hospitality, which is an act of generosity. Whether you have invited a business associate to lunch in a restaurant, a neighbor for dinner, or friends and family to a celebratory reception, your obligation is to make your guests feel comfortable in those surroundings, showing them that you sincerely appreciate their company. As

> Hospitality is making your guests feel at home, even if you wish they were.
>
> —ANONYMOUS

a result, it is up to you to do everything in consideration of your guests, particularly food preferences, both in your home or in choosing a restaurant. Remember, if you invite others to a restaurant, you are responsible for paying the bill.

Clever hosts invite people they think will enjoy each other's company and stimulate conversation. If disagreements between guests threaten to spiral out of control, especially at a dinner table, it is up to you as the host to moderate, smooth things over, and change the topic, because no guest should leave feeling embarrassed, shamed, or insulted. And while a guest might irritate you, set your annoyance aside until later. The point is to make your gathering a pleasant occasion.

Regardless of which role you happen to be playing, hospitality is a two-way street with obligations borne by both the guest and the host. What is most important to remember, however, is that coming together is a time to be social, to enjoy one another's company, to celebrate, and to connect—whether for business or pleasure, for casual gatherings or life's time-honored rituals and events. Hospitality is a gift, after all, that should be generously offered and received. When grace is lacking from either side, the gift loses its value.

37

Dress to Fit

Clothes are never a frivolity:
they always mean something.
—JAMES LAVER

Clothes don't make the man,
but clothes have got many a man a good job.
—HERBERT HAROLD VREELAND

Once upon a time, not so very long ago, there were specified dress codes for just about every occasion and setting, and, for the most part, people abided by them. People wore suits to the office, dressed up on airplanes, donned elegant clothes for parties and the theater, and conformed to particular modes of dress in school. Inappropriate attire would have been a cause for personal embarrassment.

Today, however, dress codes are much more relaxed in almost every arena. To some folks who are accustomed to more conventional attire, the laxity of standards is both irksome and, in many cases, offensive, as when clothes reveal more body parts than they cover. And while it may often be a relief not to adhere to the rigidity of the past, there are, nonetheless, situations in which moderation and guidelines are in order.

The appropriateness of our dress and appearance are important, not only because of how we may be perceived, but also because our attire can show respect and deference within a particular milieu. Although our culture has increasingly embraced individualism and self-expression through what we wear, there are times when a statement of individuality is better left unmade. For example, it is not respectful to attend a worship service dressed in an undershirt and baggy shorts that expose a butt crack. Wearing a twelve-inch skirt, a spaghetti-strap top, or a T-shirt with funny sayings is not appropriate for a corporate job interview. Showing up in casual clothing at a black-tie affair is an affront to a host. There simply are times and venues where appropriate decorum must be observed.

What to wear is a topic that I sometimes include in my Social IQ seminars, particularly as it applies to the work environment. College students accustomed to wearing jeans, torn shirts, and flip-flops sometimes resist the notion of restrictions, which they consider old-fashioned and impractical. My advice to them to is to choose a place of employment where their desired style of dress is compatible with the workplace, rather than defiantly challenging a company's dress code with noncompliant behavior.

Particularly for interviews, I recommend that candidates appear well groomed and professional, wearing clothing that is suitable for the job for which they are applying and reflective of the image they want to project. For example, a pinstriped suit may be quite appropriate for a Wall Street position but appear ridiculous for a job in a trendy fashion boutique. When in doubt, contact a company in advance about the accepted style of dress.

While some office dress codes have become more relaxed, appearance is still important because it can create an impression of your competence and professionalism. A *Newsweek* poll revealed that 202 corporate hiring managers placed *how one looks* as the third most important factor for job applicants, behind experience (#1) and confidence (#2), but above education (#4) and sense of humor (#5). Fifty-nine percent of the respondents in that same survey thought that job applicants should spend as much money on their looks as on their résumé.

For women, unfortunately, appearance is often a double-edged sword; while women have made great strides in the workforce in recent decades, the emphasis on looks is perhaps even greater than ever before. Fifty-one percent of the *Newsweek* poll respondents thought that a female applicant should dress to show off her figure. Further, Stanford law professor Deborah

> Clothes can suggest, persuade, connote, insinuate, or indeed lie, and apply subtle pressure while their wearer is speaking frankly and straightforwardly of other matters.
>
> —ANNE HOLLANDER

Rhode, former chair of the American Bar Association's Commission on Working Women and author of *The Beauty Bias*, concedes the economic effect of the beauty premium, whereby "pretty people do better." At the same time, however, some employers fire women from their jobs for being too "showy" with their bodies.

Given this paradox, it's safer to refrain from wearing clothes that are overly suggestive. Provocative attire also may deflect attention from the brains and talents that you might prefer to showcase. Bearing the *Newsweek* statistics in mind, a woman doesn't have to dress in a shapeless sack or a boxy suit—it is possible to choose clothing that is flattering and attractive as well as professional.

To young men who wish to project business savvy, I propose, at the very least, wearing trousers that are belted at the waist, along with a dress shirt that is clean and pressed, and shoes that are polished. Depending on the particular environment, you may or may not wear a suit or jacket and tie: Some companies require more formal dress while others consider it passé. When a job applicant shows up looking like he does not fit into a particular business environment, a potential employer has to decide whether the applicant is unknowingly unprofessional or simply has a flagrant disregard for expected behavior, neither of which is a desirable attribute in an employee. Although the contemporary standards and styles may be somewhat more flexible than when John Molloy first wrote *Dress for Success* a couple of decades ago, matters of dress are of no small concern. You have to look the part and act the part in order to get the part.

Regardless of the arena, how you dress can convey style, attitude, and culture, as well as your level of affluence, confidence, polish, sophistication, and professionalism. It also reflects your sensitivity to and regard for others within a particular setting or occasion. Through our clothing and appearance, we nonverbally communicate not only who we are but also how we want other people to respond to us. Our appropriate attire can reflect overall good manners as well as a sense that we are discerning and know the rules of the game. It also articulates our caring about the occasion and the people within the setting—that, ultimately, becomes a sign of respect.

38

Apologize

A great nation is like a great man:
When he makes a mistake, he realizes it.
Having realized it, he admits it.
Having admitted it, he corrects it.
He considers those who point out his faults as
his most benevolent teachers.

—LAO TZU

A stiff apology is a second insult....
The injured party does not want to be compensated
because he has been wronged; he wants to be
healed because he has been hurt.

—G. K. CHESTERTON

Like many people, my pet peeves center around petty annoyances, one being drivers who don't take their turns at traffic intersections. Recently, however, I shamefully became one of those thoughtless drivers, jumping ahead of three other cars. Within seconds, one of them chased after me, bearing down on my bumper. Moving off to the side of the road, I rolled down my window to talk to the angry man who had pulled up alongside my car. Before he could open his mouth, I apologized profusely for the same discourteous behavior of which I unabashedly accused others. The man's incensed expression melted into a smile as he said, "Think nothing of it!"

My apology was not a ploy; it was genuine. What that apology did, however, was defuse the situation and clear the air, so that each of us could get on with our days, smiling rather than fuming. Had the driver not accepted my apology so graciously, the outcome might have been very different.

Fearing such a reaction is one reason why people avoid apologizing, according to Dr. Aaron Lazare, former chancellor and dean and professor of psychiatry at the University of Massachusetts Medical School and former professor of psychiatry at Harvard and Massachusetts General Hospital. In his exquisite book *On Apology*, Lazare calls the act of offering and accepting an apology one of the most profound human interactions. He reasons, "Apologies have the power to heal humiliations and grudges, remove the desire for vengeance, and generate forgiveness on the part of the offended parties." They can both ease the fear of retaliation and diminish the guilt and shame of the offender, and, ideally, they can lead to reconciliation and repair broken relationships. He defines an apology as an encounter between two parties, in which the offender not only accepts responsibility but also expresses genuine regret or remorse to the aggrieved parties, be they individuals, families, businesses, ethnic groups, races, or nations; the apology itself can "be private or public, written or verbal, and even, at times, nonverbal."

The most crucial part of any apology, says Lazare, is the acknowledgment of the offense, which is not a cursory process. The offending behaviors need to be fully recognized and acknowledged, and the impact on the victim must be understood, as well as the breach of the social or moral contract. In addition, an apology should include an explanation; a conveyance of remorse, shame, and sincerity; and a means of reparation. What is important is that the offender is forthcoming in communicating, "I was wrong" and "It's not your fault."

There are many times, nonetheless, that apologies don't work. Lazare suggests that some reasons for failed apologies are:

- Vague or incomplete acknowledgment—*"I'm sorry for whatever I did."*
- Employing a passive voice—*"Mistakes have been made."*
- Making the apology conditional—*"If mistakes may have been made ..."*
- Querying whether there was damage to the victim—*"If anyone was hurt ..."*
- Minimizing the offense—*"There's really nothing for which to apologize."*

- Saying "I'm sorry" empathetically—*"I'm sorry you're so angry with me."*
- Identifying the wrong offense—*"I'm sorry for causing you pain, but I don't believe what I did was actually wrong."*

When an apology is delivered in the manner of any of the examples above, it can cause more harm than good because the offender has not actually accepted responsibility and blame. Learning how to make an effective and meaningful apology, thus, requires specific and concrete language as well as dedicated thought.

Another reason why people often fail to apologize, besides fearing the reaction of the offended party, is that they do not wish to appear small or diminished, lose face, or confess their shame. In courts of law, people have been reluctant in the past to apologize for fear of implying guilt. That stance may be modified somewhat in the future. Research by Jennifer Robbennolt, professor of law and psychology at the University of Illinois, shows that apologies potentially may help with the resolution of legal disputes. Providing aggrieved parties with a sense of justice and satisfaction actually can promote settlements in certain cases as well as scale down the demands for damages. Her findings show that apologies made by defendants who accept responsibility are more effective than those that merely express sympathy.

Sometimes self-justification—a process of thinking whereby an offender may not see himself as the guilty party or at fault—thwarts apologies. In the insightful *Mistakes Were Made (But Not by Me)*, authors and social psychologists Carol Tavris and Elliot Aronson argue that justifying yourself is not exactly the same thing as lying or making excuses; it is, however, lying to yourself or convincing yourself of a distortion, minimizing mistakes and bad decisions. A person can so convince himself that he actually comes to believe that his point of view or his action represents the truth; once someone goes down that path, it becomes difficult to change course.

What propels the need to justify our poor decisions and actions is a disagreeable sense called *cognitive dissonance*, a state of tension identified by social psychologist Leon Festinger more than fifty years ago. Basically, when we hold two beliefs or a belief and an action that contradict each other—such as "Eating too many sweets is bad for my diabetes" and "I eat candy every day"—the result is mental anguish, or dissonance, which we want to reduce as much as possible. That's where the justification comes in; we want to minimize the discomfort that we feel. This process can hold true for any of our opinions or beliefs. If, for instance, we receive information that is consistent with our beliefs, we think that it's a great idea; if the information is inconsistent, however, we think that it's a dumb idea. Thus, it is easy to see how cognitive dissonance potentially can affect the clarity of an offender's judgment: She filters her views so that she does not see herself as at fault or her mistake as so terrible. It is also a means of shifting blame, meaning she would not owe the aggrieved party an apology.

In his book, Dr. Lazare cites numerous apologies, some of them occurring between nations, and some offered by a nation to its people. In particular, he refers to Abraham Lincoln's Second Inaugural Address in which Lincoln apologizes for American slavery. The fight to abolish slavery, Lincoln agonizingly proclaimed, justified the Civil War, which was still being fought at the time.

Another moving example is that of Kevin Gover, assistant secretary of Indian Affairs for the U.S. Department of the Interior, who, in September 2000, delivered a heart-wrenching formal apology to Native Americans at the ceremony acknowledging the 175th anniversary of the establishment of the Bureau of Indian Affairs. Himself a Native American, Gover admitted that there was no way to ever right the wrongs of the past, but he accepted "the moral responsibility of putting things right." The fact that Gover's apology came decades after these actions occurred made it no less meaningful, which is why, even among individuals, it is never too late to apologize.

If you want the last word, apologize.

—ANONYMOUS

Many other nations have extended apologies as atonement for wrongs. Following World War II, West Germany offered profuse public apologies for its actions, including, but not limited to, ceremonial speeches, erecting monuments to the victims of the Nazis, reparations to Jews in the form of contributions to build the State of Israel, and truthful accounts in history books. By comparison, apologies made by Japan following atrocities they committed during the same war have been far less forthright and appeasing, a factor that continues to cause tension with their adversaries today.

It can be courageous and humbling to admit fault in any situation, be it an egregious offense or a small transgression, because we always run the risk that an apology will not be accepted. What I am suggesting, however, is that we each take the time to recognize not just the big mistakes we make, but also the little ways in which we hurt people and abuse them. We also need to be cognizant of times when we make someone feel small or undervalued. To say, "I didn't really mean it" or, "Everybody does it," does nothing to assuage the feelings of the hurt parties. Instead, being able to admit, "I am at fault, I apologize for what I did, and I am sorry for hurting you," then finding a way to make it better, can make all the difference.

~~ 39 ~~

Learn to Forgive

Forgiveness is not an occasional act.
It is a permanent attitude.
—MARTIN LUTHER KING JR.

Forgiveness is the sweetest revenge.
—ISAAC FRIEDMANN

During the celebration of our daughter's fourth birthday party, I committed what was, in her view, an unspeakably egregious act: I neglected to serve her the first piece of birthday cake. Worse, I did so deliberately, although with the best of intentions. The situation was that, upon blowing out the candles, Katie had specified the exact portion that she desired, which was located in the center, not along the rectangular edge. Thus, as I cut along the side of the cake, those exterior pieces were distributed to her guests; although Katie was eventually served the piece she requested, hers was not the first piece given out.

Despite my profuse explanations and humble apologies, Katie's bruised feelings did not recover from this unfortunate slight. Throughout the ensuing year, I was reminded of my indiscretion, not on a daily basis, but often enough. As her fifth birthday approached, her lament continued. Finally, frustrated by the futility of my efforts to counter my preschooler's righteous indignation with any rational persuasion, I looked at her one day and asked, "Can you forgive me?" Somewhat taken aback yet intrigued by my question, she thought for a moment, and then solemnly replied that yes, she could. Remarkably, at that point, she not only willingly forgave me, the matter never surfaced again. That simple heartfelt plea, however, has become a recurrent ritual of sorts in our household when an issue is not easily resolved or is at a stalemate. Surprisingly, it is a process that has worked, in that we've been able to put small family disputes aside, mending fences and assuaging hurt feelings.

While our familial situations usually involved lesser infractions, there are those monumental in scale, in which forgiveness may feel like an impossible act. Not surprisingly, psychologists tell us that the deeper the hurt, the more difficult it is to forgive. Nonetheless, there are shining examples of human beings who, despite enormous tragedy and suffering, have been able to forgive the unforgivable.

Etty Hillesum, a Dutch Jew who was twenty-nine years old when she perished in Auschwitz in 1943, chronicled the two years prior to her death during which she experienced the unspeakable horrors of the Nazi occupation of the Netherlands and her subsequent incarceration in Camp Westerbork. Her diaries, published almost forty years later, reveal the portrait of a woman, in the face of indescribable inhumanity, whose spirituality and faith in God increasingly deepened. Along her journey, she refused to surrender her inviolable spirit to her captors—nor did she succumb to vengeful hate and recrimination toward them. One of the last entries in her diaries reads, "After this war, two torrents will be unleashed on the world: a torrent of loving-kindness and a torrent of hatred. And then I knew: I should take the field against hatred."

Nelson Mandela, a leader in the anti-apartheid movement in South Africa, was unjustly jailed for crimes of high treason for twenty-seven years, living in a cell measuring just two square meters with one tiny window. Released from prison at the age of seventy-one, he was awarded, along with then-president F. W. de Klerk, the Nobel Peace Prize in 1993 for his efforts to peacefully bring an end to the apartheid regime and for laying the groundwork for a new democratic South Africa. In the presentation ceremony, the chairman of the Norwegian Nobel Committee noted Mandela's lack of bitterness following his incarceration, citing Mandela's own words that "he had a job to do." Later, President Clinton asked him how he was able to forgive his jailers. Mandela responded, "When I walked out of the gate I knew that if I continued to hate these people, I was still in prison."

In October 2006, in the West Nickel Mines School, an Amish one-room schoolhouse located in Lancaster County, Pennsylvania, a lone gunman entered, taking students hostage and eventually killing five girls, ages six through thirteen, and an aide, before taking his own life. In the days that followed, an awestruck nation witnessed the response of the Amish community to the massacre. Rather than seeking retribution, the community members preached love and forgiveness for the murderer, Charles Roberts. Their wish was to emulate the teachings of Jesus about what we must do when bearing terrible suffering, as well as to reach out, not only to the families who had lost children but also to the family of the killer. Embracing Charles Roberts's father, one Amish neighbor declared, "We will forgive you."

These are but three examples of souls who endured devastating hurt but did not allow their victimization to consume them with lifelong bitterness. Instead, they exhibited their strength and humanity by embracing love, peace, hope, and joy. As a result, they were liberated and empowered by forgiving those who had inflicted deep harm, letting go of resentment and any inclination for revenge.

Many world religions teach us to practice forgiveness as faithful followers of their spiritual teachings. Yet, forgiveness is not something that you can force just by saying the words. Studies have shown that simply deciding to forgive someone doesn't work well; it is more effective to draw on a process involving love, compassion, and empathy. And although University of California, Riverside, psychologist Sonja Lyubomirsky enumerates practicing forgiveness as one of twelve scientifically based strategies that can boost happiness, she clearly admits that it can be one of the more challenging to carry out because it requires a great deal of effort and practice.

Why is that? Some people perceive forgiveness as a sign of weakness, giving away power and allowing the other person to get away with something. Also, in the short term, anger, resentment, and fear are protective measures that help us manage and cope, keeping the exposure to further hurt, or the person who hurt us, at bay. We hold on to those emotions because it makes us feel justified in our feelings toward the transgressor, who has wronged us. However, in the long term, those emotions can do more harm to us than to the person to whom they are directed.

> To forgive is to set a prisoner free and discover that the prisoner was you.
>
> —LEWIS B. SMEDES

Research tells us that there are enormous mental, physical, and social benefits when we forgive others. More than fourteen hundred scientific studies have shown that those who successfully practice forgiveness have reduced anger and hostility, lower levels of stress hormones and depression, and a lower incidence of drug and substance abuse, and are less neurotic and narcissistic. Forgiveness releases us from the bonds of dwelling on our hurts, playing the events over and over in our heads, so that we are able to move on with our lives. Further, forgiveness deepens our sense of humanity and empathy, helps us reestablish closeness in our relationships, and increases our prosocial desire to help others.

It is important to clarify the way in which psychologists who study forgiveness define the process, because many people misunderstand the concept, according to University of Wisconsin psychologist Robert Enright, in his book *Forgiveness Is a Choice*. First, reconciliation with the transgressor is not a requisite factor; forgiveness, for example, might be extended to a person who is no longer even alive. Forgiveness also does not imply forgetting, because it is a deliberate act; if we simply forget, we cannot be in a position to purposefully forgive. It also is not a matter of excusing, condoning, pardoning (in a legal sense), trusting, or waiving judicial proceedings or financial reparations. Because it is a deliberate action, forgiveness must be faced head-on, directly and completely.

Forgiveness is an individual process; there is no single path to achieving that objective. There are some for whom reconciliation with the transgressor is important, while to others it is not. Also, some people are more inclined to forgive than others, with young children being the least likely and older adults the most likely. Some psychologists point to an apology as the greatest predictor of forgiveness; however, the effectiveness may depend on the richness of the apology, with genuine remorse being a key factor.

Forgiveness is not an insipid act: It often requires great love, courage, and empathy. Forgiveness also is not a process that happens overnight; it may well take a long time, particularly if we thoughtfully progress through phases like those delineated in Enright's book. However, it must be heartfelt. It is a gift that should be given freely, without strings. Once you do forgive, it is a gift to the offender, but also to yourself.

Celebrate Diversity

> If we cannot end our differences, at least we can
> help make the world safe for diversity.
> —PRESIDENT JOHN F. KENNEDY

> He prayed—it wasn't my religion.
> He ate—it wasn't what I ate.
> He spoke—it wasn't my language.
> He dressed—it wasn't what I wore.
> He took my hand—it wasn't the color of mine.
> But when he laughed—it was how I laughed,
> And when he cried—it was how I cried.
> —SIXTEEN-YEAR-OLD AMY MADDOX
> OF BARGERSVILLE, INDIANA

A few years ago, I attempted to undertake a project, which I referred to as Family Feasts and Celebrations. Through a book and accompanying film series, my intent was to depict people around the world celebrating their respective cultures and beliefs through the rituals of their lives. My real hope was that by opening our minds and learning about one another, we could develop a greater awareness, understanding, and acceptance of all people in the world. Although limited resources made it impossible to bring this project to fruition, a seminal message of this book is about connecting with all of humanity, recognizing that we are one.

In a small room in my church hangs a tiny hand-stitched work of embroidery that says, "God looks at hearts the way that we look at faces." If we could employ that sublime vision, going beneath a person's skin, we would discover that each of us has a beating human heart, pumping blood that courses through our veins. We also might see how we share similar feelings, love for our children, hopes, expectations, dreams, dislikes, pain, and disappointments. Further, we might realize our shared physical commonalities as human beings living on the same planet—how each of us thirsts, hungers, and breathes. And if we talked, we might get to know people as they really are, rather than who we think they are; it might even surprise us to learn how many of us have peaceful motives that have nothing to do with those of our respective leaders.

Sadly, too often we focus on what divides and disconnects rather than what unites us. Our vision becomes narrowly constrained, clouded by prejudiced beliefs, derogatory stereotypes, bigotry, hatred, discrimination, and ignorance that limit our view of humanity. We label people who we think are not like us, rather than considering them as human beings, just like us.

When we celebrate diversity, however, we experience a tapestry of humankind, woven with rich, heterogeneous, and multicultural threads, derived from race, religion, gender, age, ethnicity, nationality, marital status, socioeconomic status, intelligence, handicaps, sexual orientation, organization memberships, political views, life experiences, interests, and so forth. Even height, weight, and the color of our eyes are categories by which we are grouped. As we "cross-reference" our commonalities, we bridge a connection to other human beings, realizing that it is not possible to be a member of only one group or classification: Each of us belongs to multiple groups. I, for instance, am female, a wife, a mother, a church member, a United States citizen, a baby boomer, a business owner, a writer, and more, all at once. However, I cannot be *only* a woman or *only* a boomer. What makes us truly unique is what we think and do, and how we connect to or separate ourselves from others.

> In each of us, there is a little of all of us.
>
> —GEORG C. LICHTENBERG

If we are ever to banish our divides, it might be helpful to ask ourselves what so threatens us that we are driven to hate or ostracize certain people. Sometimes we make judgments about people we don't even know; once we meet them, our opinions and feelings may change. One very powerful example is Peace It Together, a project that, in 2006 and 2008, brought together teenagers from Canada, Israel, and Palestine, who collaborated by making fifteen films within two three-week periods. The result was not simply the production of an array of quality films but also the extraordinary friendships and deeper understandings that came about through the teenagers' communication and proximity to those of other cultures.

I'm not suggesting that we have to like everybody. However, we can make a conscious effort to respect one another and do no harm to those whom we may like less, preserving the dignity of each human being. Even Mother Teresa once remarked, "Jesus said love one another. He didn't say love the whole world."

We can start by accepting that each and every one of us has a right to live and be on this planet. From there, we can ponder how we can peacefully coexist in this world, altering our thinking and our actions. The *we* begins with *you* and *me*, as together we take one step at a time.

Travel Often and Well

The real voyage of discovery consists not in seeking
new landscapes but in having new eyes.
—MARCEL PROUST

When you travel, remember that a foreign country
is not designed to make you comfortable.
It is designed to make its own people comfortable.
—CLIFTON FADIMAN

Growing up, I always had an insatiable desire to travel. Fortunately, I married a man who shared my passion, so that when our daughter was born, we bundled her up and brought her along from babyhood on.

When I once told a friend that we had just returned with our two-and-a-half-year-old from a trip to France and Italy, my friend retorted, "She'll never remember any of it!" Suddenly, I had a flash of memories from our trip—Katie playing on a beach with a child whose language she did not speak, Katie munching on fresh anchovies in a restaurant, Katie sleeping in her stroller while we wheeled her around, in and out of village shops. Pondering a moment, I finally said, "What Katie will remember is that she doesn't always have to be in a familiar environment, eat the same food, have the same routine, or sleep in her own bed. If she can be open to adventure and learn to adapt to different surroundings at this early age, she will have learned valuable life lessons."

Travel offers an incomparable educational experience, particularly if you are fueled by curiosity and open to the excitement of discovery. It's not just an opportunity to visit landmarks and tour new vistas; it is a way to learn about different people, understand their respective cultures, and discern the factors that shape their lives.

It is the unfortunate traveler who expects everything to be the way it is at home, and seeks only what is familiar. While fast-food chains have pro-liferated everywhere, it's a pity to go to a region so different from your own and not sample the indigenous foods. And though no one can be fluent in every language, it is helpful to learn at least a few words or phrases—espe-cially *hello*, *please*, and *thank you*—which expresses an appreciation of and an interest in others and helps, in a small way, to make a connection.

If you are going to learn about the people, it pays to research local cus-toms beforehand so that you neither risk offending others nor are offended by them. Keep in mind that *they* are not odd if they don't behave exactly like you. Direct eye contact, for instance, is a sign of respect, earnestness, interest, and self-confidence in the United States but not in many Asian, Latino, and Caribbean cultures, where it can be a sign of disrespect for eld-ers and those of greater authority. In Western cultures, staring at people is very impolite; however, in India, staring at others is accepted as normal curiosity. Indians are also not sensitive to bodily noises and expulsions of air. In China, it is considered a compliment to burp or slurp soup.

In America, we express our enjoyment and compliment our host by cleaning our plate; in Cambodia, however, it is a sign that you desire more. In the Philippines, Thailand, and Jordan, it is polite to leave a small por-tion of food as a sign that the host has provided abundantly. And while it is a sign of respect to remove your shoes when entering a Japanese home, be careful how you sport those shoes in the Middle East, because it is deeply insulting to point the soles toward an individual's face.

We all must remember that none of us is above paying attention to customs and protocol. Colors can carry deep symbolic meanings, spreading good will or bad depending on what you wear. When Pope Benedict visited the White House, First Lady Laura Bush made a faux pas by wearing a white suit, a color worn only by His Holiness when you're in his presence. Touching others can also be taboo in many cultures. First Lady Michelle Obama learned that lesson firsthand when she was introduced at Buckingham Palace, because even she was not supposed to touch the queen!

As you travel, observe what factors may have influenced the lifestyle of a foreign land. Did geography create barriers or make the country vulnerable to attack? Were trade routes accessible, giving rise to commerce and exposure to the outside world, or was the country isolated, slowing its development? How do climate and soil determine agriculture and choice of food? In the Australian Outback, water is so scarce that it is a major factor in limiting population; a grub worm is a viable source of protein because the arid land has little animal or plant life.

Discern socioeconomic factors, whether there is a thriving middle class or whether the population is educated. When Eleanor Roosevelt traveled the United States on behalf of her husband, President Franklin Roosevelt—whose mobility was curtailed by his crippled legs—he instructed her to note the local housing, but also what was hanging on the clotheslines. FDR advised that you learn a lot about people and their standard of living just by looking at the clothes hanging out to dry. Similarly, I like to explore local goods and designs. Once, in Cairo, I ventured into an Egyptian shopping center. Wandering into an appliance store, I learned a lot just by observing the level of sophistication of the washing machines and refrigerators. A curling iron in the beauty parlor was straight out of the 1930s as it sizzled my hair, sending out wafts of smoke. Although the pyramids and pharaohs' tombs were impressive, I confess to remembering more about modern-day than ancient Egypt.

> The world is a book and those who do not travel read only one page.
>
> —ST. AUGUSTINE

What role does religion play in a country? Are there strict controls, or is it a secular society? Are there visible rituals, such as making temple offerings to the gods or a call to prayer five times a day? On a trip to Bali, my husband and I were fortunate to be invited to the funeral of a high local official who had recently passed away. Assuming that it would be a subdued and somber affair, like funerals are here, we respectfully chose not to bring a video camera, considering it intrusive. As we soon discovered, this was a celebration to which almost every person on the island had been invited, including tourists. The funeral procession was a magnificent parade, with family members wearing colorful symbolic costumes and masks. The casket was transported on a bier topped by a tiered tower, bedecked with tall umbrellas trimmed with red fringe, requiring the removal of the roadside electrical wires. It was all part of a Hindu ceremony followed by cremation. This spectacular rite was in sharp contrast to the simple one we had witnessed a year earlier in Nepal, in which the funeral pyre consisted of a raft that, bearing a body, peacefully floated down the river, all in flame.

Intuitively, you can discern the general moods of the native people simply by being sensitive to the surroundings. Many years ago, we stumbled into the Arab section of a West Bank town where Israeli settlements were being built: Immediately, we felt a strong air of tension, as the locals' suspicion of us was evident. Departing quickly, we learned soon thereafter that a ten-year-old Israeli girl had been stoned to death three days earlier. On a visit to the former Yugoslavia, we found little joy or laughter among the people, who wore dour facial expressions. We concluded that they didn't seem to like each other very much. Within a couple of years, the country was war-torn and subsequently broken apart as a result of ancient religious hatred.

History, as well as the present day, comes alive through travel. It is both a joy and a privilege to experience a culture with new eyes—*your own*. Long-held notions dissolve, as you gain an understanding of why people live and believe as they do. You can make similar observations in your own country, determining whether or not locals venture more than twenty-five miles from where they were born, for they might not know much about you! Many contend that there would be fewer wars if people traveled and learned more about other cultures.

Mark Twain once said, "Travel is fatal to prejudice, bigotry, and narrow-mindedness." Through travel, we are more apt to develop genuine respect for people and their beliefs; it opens our minds and connects us to the world at large, which brings me back to my opening story. As a preschooler, our daughter could not possibly understand the nuances of different cultures. However, our intent was both to share our passion and to help her learn to cope with new and different surroundings at an early age so that she would not be hindered by a fear of logistics and other stumbling blocks to travel later in life. Through early exposure, our hope was not only to build her self-confidence in this way, but also to instill in her a love of exploration and a sense of curiosity about people and the world. As I said, if she could begin to do that while she was young, she would learn valuable lifelong lessons.

∾ 42 ∾

Consider Your
Fellow Travelers

But why, oh why, do the wrong people travel,
when the right people stay at home?
—NOEL COWARD

If an ass goes traveling,
he'll not come home a horse.
—THOMAS FULLER

Travel today, regardless of the destination or mode of transportation, is stressful. Security lines, quart bags of carry-on liquids, tight seating, add-on fees, and delays compound the stress, making any journey less pleasurable than it once was. However, heightened awareness, respect, and consideration of our fellow travelers along the way helps ease situations where flaring tempers are apt to rise.

A "rudeness poll" of 1,600 participants in a Travelocity survey noted that the most "disliked passengers" were seatmates with poor hygiene and those who coughed and sneezed. Roughly half the respondents complained about misbehaving children, particularly those who kicked the backs of the seats in front of them or who were allowed to run up and down the aisles without supervision. Also annoying were passengers who took up most of the plane's overhead bin space with their "stuff" as well as travelers who tried to deplane first, shoving those ahead of them.

It is important to remember that travel personnel, such as those behind the ticket counter and flight attendants, are often beleaguered by the bad behavior of passengers, as well as the additional workload brought on by cutbacks in personnel and other areas. They are not servants. (A flight attendant friend of mine was once so mistreated—like a dog—by a passenger, that he got down on all fours in the aisle and barked like one. I think he got his point across.) Likewise, keep in mind that hotel housekeeping staff are not your personal maids. Even if you don't do it at home, keep your room and personal belongings in a tidy manner.

Good company in a journey makes the way seem shorter.

—IZAAK WALTON

As airlines begin to allow Internet access, be mindful that the use of your computer does not disrupt your seatmates, particularly in regard to sound, which can be controlled by using earphones. Further, on a train or plane, do not take up "more than your share" of space by setting up a mobile office, whereby your papers, laptop, and cell-phone calls infringe on other passengers. Be sensitive to those next to you who may prefer to sleep or read rather than talk to strangers; if you do strike up a conversation, keep your voice low.

Lastly, pay attention to what is happening around you. If you notice a person struggling with hoisting a bag into a bin or overhead rack and are physically able to lend a hand, then do just that. Moreover, unless you are frail, elderly, or pregnant, offer your bus or train seat to someone who is. Remember that how well you travel on a trip should be no different from how you travel through life.

43

Practice Nonviolence

History's worst atrocities were
carried out in good faith.
—ANTHONY DE MELLO, SJ

Violence comes in many more forms than can ever be described in a chapter ...

> ... wars between countries, religions, and street gangs

> ... physical assaults on people and their property

> ... aggression on highways and in sports arenas

> ... verbal abuse between spouses, parents, and children

> ... bullying in schools and on the Internet

> ... environments of fear created by tyrannical despots

> ... denial of human rights and justice

Assuming a mantle of nonviolence does not mean sitting back and doing nothing, nor does it imply a lack of fortitude or commitment to resist situations involving inhumanity. Instead, nonviolent resistance requires a special form of courage and confrontation, as well as enormous self-restraint. Violence always begets more violence. It will never resolve any conflict with your family, friends, or neighbors. Choose to act with kindness and compassion instead.

There have been many notable persons who have dedicated their lives to the mission of nonviolence as a peaceful means of resistance. May their lives and powerful words inspire you.

There are many causes I would die for. There is not a single cause I would kill for.

—MOHANDAS GANDHI

Nonviolence means avoiding not only external physical violence but also internal violence of spirit. You not only refuse to shoot a man, but you refuse to hate him.

—MARTIN LUTHER KING JR.

Peace cannot be kept by force. It can only be achieved by understanding.

—ALBERT EINSTEIN

Nonviolence is not inaction. It is not discussion. It is not for the timid or weak. Nonviolence is hard work. It is the willingness to sacrifice. It is the patience to win.

—CÉSAR CHÁVEZ

You can't shake hands with a clenched fist.

—INDIRA GANDHI

If you want to make peace with your enemy, you have to work with your enemy. Then he becomes your partner.

—NELSON MANDELA

We must not allow ourselves to become like the system we oppose.

—ARCHBISHOP DESMOND TUTU

44

Judge Not
Thy Neighbor

Any fool can criticize, condemn, and complain—
and most fools do.

—DALE CARNEGIE

Human beings are fallible. One demonstration of our own fallibility is in the way that we criticize, judge, and even condemn other people and their circumstances, sometimes instantly, without any knowledge of their situation. Our error in this regard is threefold. First, we *presume* to know what is going on in their lives, even though we don't. Second, we don't stop to question whether we could be wrong or whether our information is flawed. Third, our tendency to conjecture in this manner may influence others in a negative way, particularly our children, who may develop similar shortsighted critical thinking patterns.

Sometimes our criticism and judgment are based on a single incident or occurrence; other times they are based on a prejudice held over a lifetime. In any event, unfounded recrimination gets in the way of our ability to keep an open mind and see clearly. Too often, such judgments and opinions are based on insufficient or mistaken knowledge. For example:

- Mocking someone's clothing as cheap without knowing that the loss of his job has forced a meager existence.
- Referring to a coworker as "stuck up" because she is standoffish, without realizing that she suffers from shyness and low self-esteem.

Sometimes, we label and stereotype people based on long-held beliefs or prejudices, such as:

- Profiling people along racial or ethnic lines.
- Criticizing obese people because they eat too much (while also assuming that they are incompetent or indigent).

Consider, for example, *To Kill a Mockingbird*, in which a lesson for the main character in the book is also intended for the reader.

The story is narrated and viewed through the eyes of Scout, a young girl growing up in a small southern town in the 1930s. The novel focuses on white prejudice against African Americans, illustrated through the trial of a black man falsely accused of raping a white woman. A subplot, however, revolves around another form of prejudice, depicted in Scout's perception of Boo Radley, a mysterious neighbor with somewhat aberrant and peculiar behavior, whom Scout imagines to be a monster. As Scout both fears and ridicules Boo behind his back, her wise father, Atticus, advises her and her brother, Jem, that we never really know a man until we stand in his shoes and walk around in them. At the end of the story, Boo is venerated in Scout's

If you judge, investigate.

—SENECA

eyes as he ultimately saves the children's lives. Scout sees that Boo, far from being a mysterious monster, is a kind and gentle soul. This knowledge allows her to overcome her original prejudice—which had been based on ignorance—and befriend him. While Scout might never know what it is like to walk in Boo's shoes, the sage counsel of Atticus is underscored in that we have no right to sit in judgment of others when we have no knowledge of their circumstances or point of view.

The lesson for all of us is to recognize the fallacy and repercussions of our snap judgments: There might be more to the story than we could possibly ever imagine. Therefore, rather than drawing firm conclusions, our first task is to consider what we might not know before we criticize, judge, or condemn.

45

Play Fair and Everyone Wins

What really matters is not just our own winning
but helping other people to win, too.
—FRED ROGERS

Fairness is what justice really is.
—POTTER STEWART

Fairness is one of the pillars that play an essential role in how we develop our interpersonal relationships, structure organizations, live amicably in communities, and function as a democracy. In short, along with justice, it is a cornerstone of civilization. Determining what is *right* or *fair*, however, is not always easy, particularly when our subjective truth is filtered by those murky shades of gray that color our point of view, causing us to tip the scales in our favor.

We live in a culture, however, where too often winning at all costs takes precedence, regardless of who we hurt in the process. It's not enough to compete or play fairly; the real winner is the one who pummels an opponent into the dirt or takes unfair advantage of the other party. For instance, the buyer of a house who squeezes the lowest price out of a distressed widow is considered savvy, or the negotiator who disguises the fine print is judged as clever. An executive who may have run a company into the ground can still earn a severance package greater than the endowment of a large university. Although the movie *Wall Street*'s Gordon Gekko was fictional, his view of fairness is evidenced throughout our society, whereby winning is a zero-sum game—either you win or you lose.

When fairness prevails, the solutions benefit both parties and involve shared responsibility and a cooperative spirit; compromise is often an integral component. Such solutions are at the core of national treaties, congressional legislation, and major business dealings. However, conflicts also occur on a daily basis in our own lives: We become the arbiters of what is fair and how

> It is much more difficult to know what is fair than what is unfair.
>
> —MICHAEL JOSEPHSON

the "account" is settled. In many cases, the fair solution to a conflict is not always a clear-cut choice. For example, think about what you would consider the fair approach in these hypothetical scenarios:

- Is a customer whose old but expensive suit is ruined by a dry cleaner entitled to partial reimbursement or replacement of the garment?

- What stand does a high school administration—with a policy of zero tolerance for vandalism—take against an honors student, about to graduate, whose prank causes disruption but no real harm or damage?

- Should a sales manager who contributes heavily to the bottom line, but also humiliates employees under him, be fired or allowed to continue in the same manner?

Striving for fairness comes from a sincere desire to consider the other person's position and encompasses a conscious concern and respect for the other party. Above all, it is a recognition that you don't need to win everything in order to win. Helping others win is more than an act of generosity; it is a bridge that engenders good feelings and cooperation in a civilized society.

46

Put All Hands on Deck

We live in a world in which we need to share
responsibility. It's easy to say, "It's not my child, not
my community, not my world, not my problem."
Then there are those who see the need and respond.
I consider those people my heroes.

—FRED ROGERS

We cannot live only for ourselves.
A thousand fibers connect us with our fellow men.

—HERMAN MELVILLE

It is said that "it takes a village" to raise a child. The reality is that it also takes a village of energized and vested individuals to create, establish, and *grow* any community, be it a neighborhood, a religious institution, an organization, a business, a government, a town, a nation, or the world at large. We cannot expect any entity to thrive based on an assumption that "someone else will do the job." It is vital for each of us to do our part. We cannot presume, for example, that our religious home will always be there if and when we need it if we don't contribute financially to its ongoing operations or participate as a member of the congregation. We can't expect a local referendum that we favor to pass if we don't get out and vote. Nor will our energy consumption diminish unless we are willing to make individual sacrifices. We have the choice, and the privilege, to jump in and participate.

There are untold positive results when members of a community are on board. For instance, schools are better, with higher levels of student learning, when parents share responsibility for education with teachers and administrators. Local neighborhoods are made safer through community watch programs. We often get better consumer products or changes in laws thanks to the efforts of advocacy groups. The green movement, for example, is in full swing, thanks to collective recycling efforts and a commitment to protect our environment. Victims of natural disasters obtain relief due to the generosity and aid of outsiders.

Local and global problems demand our attention and intervention. It may sometimes feel like many of the problems that beset others have no bearing on our lives. However, it is important to understand the impact and rippling repercussions of these issues on our society.

Society is at its worst when we refuse to get involved. One March night in 1964, Kitty Genovese, a twenty-eight-year-old woman, was stabbed to death by an assailant only one hundred feet from the front door of her apartment complex in Queens, New York. Residents in her building heard her screams for help, but no one came to her aid or called the police. The event was labeled the "bystander effect" by social psychologists, meaning that the greater the number of people present, the less likely they were to offer help. (What occurs is a diffusion of responsibility: People who are witnessing an emergency or a disastrous event assume that someone else will help. Inversely, when there are fewer people present, there is a greater likelihood that they will offer assistance.)

> Doing nothing for others is the undoing of ourselves.
>
> —HORACE MANN

We could cite numerous other atrocities throughout history in which citizens chose to look the other way rather than get involved. The Holocaust is one extreme example: Villagers living within close proximity of the concentration camps did nothing to help the brutally tortured and murdered souls imprisoned behind the barbed wire.

There are thousands of ways in which each of us can get involved and participate in community, and none of us gets off the hook if we want the world to be a better place. Are you passionate about an unfilled need in your community? Become a leader and organize your own group. If, for instance, there is a lack of organic vegetables in your area, organize a farmers' market or community co-op garden. Find ways to be creative!

Besides, when we all work together and share responsibility, we have a better chance of succeeding, be it in educating our children, feeding the hungry, or preserving human rights. We just need to roll up our sleeves and get our hands dirty.

So, see a need? See what you can do!

47

Choose Your Heroes Wisely

> Keep your eyes on the stars,
> and your feet on the ground.
> —THEODORE ROOSEVELT

> Heroes are created by popular demand, sometimes
> out of the scantiest materials, or none at all.
> —GERALD WHITE JOHNSON

Given the stuff of which reality TV, gossip columns, and political campaigns are made, dignity and decorum often pale in comparison, failing to capture our attention.

Addicted to sensationalism, we flock, like moths to a flame, to incidents of celebrities behaving badly, with their antics drawing more attention than their accomplishments. Under the guise of our right to know, we dig for dirt in the lives of public figures and officials, titillated by the latest, juiciest scandal. The famous can become the infamous, thanks to the media lens; seduced by their allure, unfortunately, we often mistake those in the spotlight for role models.

There is a danger, however, for us as well as for the celebrities, when that light is shined so brightly. We immortalize sports icons, elevating them to godlike status, only to be surprised and disappointed by their flaws. And when the sexual escapades of lofty political officials are unexpectedly uncovered, we doubt their integrity overall, allowing their failings to overshadow any previous career accomplishments.

While fame is alluring, it is also illusory, particularly when its endurance is dependent on a fickle public. Genuine heroes, however, reflect a depth of character or accomplishment, possessing qualities that we admire and wish that we ourselves had. We wonder, for example, if we could summon the same courage as the firefighters on 9/11 who trudged into the burning Twin Towers. Could we serve the desperately poor, as did Mother Teresa, pursue the training rigors of Olympic athletes, evoke the wisdom of Abraham Lincoln, or lead Great Britain as Winston Churchill did during her darkest hour?

A person does not have to be a figure of national or international stature to be a hero. Philip Zimbardo, Stanford University professor emeritus of psychology, promotes a concept he calls the "banality of heroism," which is rooted in the notion that "we are all potential heroes waiting for a moment in life to perform a heroic deed." This idea debunks the myth that heroism stems from superhuman characteristics; rather, it is a universal attribute within the reach of every one of us. To this end, Zimbardo has created a program called "Heroic Imagination," intended to foster and develop each person's own heroic idea. "Heroes," says Zimbardo, "put compassion to work," committing their "best selves" in support of others. Although scientists do not yet know why some people act while others do not in any given situation, through the research and educational efforts of this program in schools and elsewhere, it is hoped that more people will be inspired to answer the call.

Such bravery is found among ordinary people who lead everyday lives and often don't think of themselves as heroes. When fifty-year-old Wesley Autrey was asked why he jumped onto the New York City subway tracks in 2007 to save a stranger from being killed by an oncoming train, his response was that he simply did what any human being would do for another. However, heroic deeds are not limited to valiant acts like rescuing people from burning buildings or battlefields. Having the courage to make moral choices and do the right thing—regardless of the personal sacrifices or consequences involved—is what makes a hero. A hero may be the whistle-blower whose courage allows her to stand up to corruption, or to rise up on the side of right when any other action or inaction would be wrong. It may be the teenager who defies his peers and defends a friend against a bully or the threat of malicious gossip and lies, or a single parent who works sixty-hour weeks scrubbing floors so she can send her kid to college. These heroic acts may not attract celebrity-style attention and fame; however, theirs is admirable behavior worth emulating.

Considering some celebrities and their exploits, it may well be better to let some icons be bygones.

48

Enhance Your Likeability

Basically, likeability comes down to creating positive emotional experiences in others. When you make others feel good, they tend to gravitate to you.

—TIM SANDERS

Shopping in a hardware store is, generally, something I do only out of necessity, not pleasure. That was my long-held practice until recently, when I discovered a store where the service is not just friendly but delightful. Beginning with Charlie, the honey-colored mutt that greets me at the door, my shopping experience is satisfying, so much so that I am compelled to return. Even if my purchase is small, I am treated as a valued customer whose questions are patiently answered by the staff. When I once complimented the owner on the congenial atmosphere, he responded, "You have to work in life at being miserable."

His reply made me consider how many of us do work at being miserable, wearing sour expressions that exude negativity, even when life, at the moment, is relatively good. We've all known those grumpy, whining, complaining, disagreeable souls whom we keep at arm's length, lest their bad moods rub off on us. There are also people who simply aren't nice—nasty, obnoxious, or abusive—who make us feel bad about ourselves so that we avoid them at all costs. In either case, such personalities are unlikeable, which, in turn, isolates the poor individuals who bear this countenance. Some of us, who fear being trod upon like doormats, assert, "Nice guys finish last." If this is your view, think again, because strong evidence points to the contrary. Tim Sanders, author of *The Likeability Factor*, presents substantial research documenting the numerous advantages that likeable people have over those who are not. One such study, conducted by Yale University and the Center for Socialization and Development, noted that the most successful leaders, from corporate CEOs to PTA presidents, made a sincere effort to be liked, coupled with their respectful treatment of subordinates. The study went on to say that, unlike other species in the animal kingdom that gain success through aggression, people are more likely to achieve it by being nice. Research has shown that people who are likeable are more likely to have others listen to and remember them; the same goes for the advertising messages of preferred products. Likeability also helps build trust.

Likeable people are generally more popular and successful in life and in business, having more lucrative careers and greater opportunities for advancement. Their harmonious working relationships make them more productive, motivating others to do well. They are less likely to be downsized from their jobs, and, as political candidates, they are more likely to be elected to office. Doctors and other service providers spend more time with those who are friendly and likeable. They garner more respect and recognition, not just at work, but also in classrooms, because teachers favor students who are likeable. Even among family members, likeability plays a key role as a predictor of more successful marriages as well as better relationships between parents and children.

Likeability in relationships is important because it affects, over time, how you make others feel, conveying your interest in others, in addition to treating them well. Sanders lists four factors that contribute to likeability:

1. *Friendliness*—whereby you express a *liking* for another person; this quality is essential in getting along with others.

2. *Relevance*—how you *connect* with other people's interests, wants, and needs.

3. *Empathy*—your capacity to understand the feelings, motivations, and situations of others.

4. *Realness*—genuine qualities that make you authentic and down-to-earth, as opposed to hypocrisy, dishonesty, and insincerity.

As you develop these traits, your "L-Factor" (likeability factor) goes up, concomitantly increasing your potential to extend and deepen relationships with others.

> I suppose leadership at one time meant muscles; but today, it means getting along with people.
>
> —MOHANDAS GANDHI

Friendliness and likeability also go a long way toward greasing the skids in life, forging alliances with those with whom you may have disagreements. President Ronald Reagan, for example, was known for his skill in reaching across the aisle to political opponents as a way of building consensus on legislation that he favored. While Reagan firmly stood his ground during business hours, after five o'clock partisan differences fell by the wayside as he easily mingled with cohorts on the opposite side of the aisle. Even his bitter enemies found the guy so darned likeable!

Liking others and showing genuine interest in them is a positive way that we *connect* with the world around us, building relationships through mutual sharing of interests, needs, and feelings. It is hard to feign being likeable, because phoniness will inevitably be unmasked. Given that most of us want to be liked, becoming likeable is something that we can intentionally put our minds to, using Sanders's guidelines. Chances are, the more we grow our "L-Factor," the more we may just like ourselves!

49

Work at Workplace Civility

> If everyone is moving forward together,
> then success takes care of itself.
> —HENRY FORD

> If you drink much from a bottle marked "poison,"
> it is almost certain to disagree with you, sooner or later.
> —LEWIS CARROLL,
> *ALICE'S ADVENTURES IN WONDERLAND*

Civility—conduct whereby people treat each other with respect, courtesy, and consideration—is one of the most positive and sustaining attributes that can ever be ingrained in a job setting. An atmosphere of pervasive civility, imbued with affirmative attitudes, can enhance and nurture virtually every operational aspect of a workplace—leadership and management; team building; employee morale, motivation, performance, and sense of pride; job satisfaction; productivity; and customer relationships. In short, civility undergirds the achievement of overall excellence in any company, organization, or institution.

Conversely, when the workplace exudes an undercurrent of incivility, the entire workplace is affected, casting a toxic pall that weighs upon and seeps into every crevice. Interpersonal relationships suffer, as do creativity and productivity. Incivility acts as a savage and devastating force that sweeps through the work environment, resulting in heightened unhappiness and stress, which then leads to conflict, employee health problems, absenteeism, and tardiness. Negative emotions and toxic attitudes rule the day. Anger, fear, hostility, suspicion, mistrust, contempt, and criticism undermine any positive efforts toward building openness and trust.

While most of us would prefer an atmosphere of civility, workers often don't have a choice, or at least any immediate means of escape. We get stuck in a job, which, however unpleasant, provides a paycheck that we desperately need in order to live. There are no easy outs.

Many business owners and corporate heads are, perhaps, unenlightened about the harmful repercussions of incivility on a company's staff, customers, productivity, and profits. Maybe they are unaware of their own officious demeanor. Or they may hold on to abusive managers who are, otherwise, considered too valuable to lose.

Unfortunately, incivility at work is partly an extension of the overall culture of rudeness. Admittedly, there is no "one size fits all" solution: The issue is complex, with an array of causes and effects. Further complicating the problem, the levels of uncivil behaviors can range from the aggressive, such as blinding rage, bullying, and humiliating others, to more passive and covert behaviors, such as excluding others, taking credit for someone else's work, or merely rolling your eyes in disagreement.

Professors Christine Pearson and Christine Porath, authors of *The Cost of Bad Behavior: How Incivility Is Damaging Your Business and What to Do about It*, showcase five companies that serve as role models of workplace civility policies. While the strategies and styles of the companies differed, the researchers noted that each of their successes came about by means of consistent small steps, which is how a civil workplace is created and sustained. Also of significance is that, in each case study, the civility policy flowed from the top down, filtering through all levels, permeating the entire structure. Executives model the culture and the ideals; employees are hired who *fit* the belief system. Civility is the norm, not an aberration or an afterthought, with a prevailing culture of mutual respect and inclusivity. Employees are valued. Incivility is not tolerated. If an employee has a complaint, there is someone to whom he can complain and a system in place to redress the problem. What is so encouraging is that, in

> Attitude is a little thing that makes a big difference.
>
> —WINSTON CHURCHILL

each of these companies, their respective system not only works but also has produced untold rewards and successes, in terms of employee satisfaction, retention, and productivity, as well as the bottom line.

Renowned restaurateur Danny Meyer has achieved extraordinary success and maintained a nearly unparalleled level of excellence based on his commitment to "enlightened hospitality." Author of *Setting the Table: The Transforming Power of Hospitality in Business*, Meyer maintains that "service is a *monologue*," whereas "hospitality is a *dialogue*." Customers are *heard* and treated equally, regardless of the price they pay for a bottle of wine. Empathy with a customer, says Meyer, is essential, as are self-awareness and integrity, which, he claims, require us to be accountable for doing the right thing. Meyer's business model is based on a "virtuous cycle," in which the goodwill from one level feeds into the next.

The model begins with trusted and optimistic employees, team players who, because they take pride in their work, joyfully serve the customer— the second level of the cycle. Customers, from the time they make a phone reservation to the end of the meal, are made to feel that they are cared for and matter. Next in the virtuous cycle is the community, in which Meyer invests heavily, locally and nationally, through organizations such as Share Our Strength, a national nonprofit dedicated to ending hunger in the United States. Aware that a restaurant's food cannot be stellar without trusted suppliers—the fourth element of the cycle—Meyer cultivates supplier relationships based on integrity, loyalty, and trust. And while he is interested in making a profit for his investors—the fifth part of the cycle— Meyer maintains that he has always focused his attention on hospitality and serving the customer, rather than on the bottom line.

The principles of good behavior and getting along with people are no different at work than in any other aspect of life. Your colleagues may not be people whom you would choose as friends; you might not particularly even *like* them. Nonetheless, it is imperative to develop respectful and workable relationships. Having a positive attitude encourages cooperation, collaboration, and motivation; combined with a willingness to accept responsibility and do your share, a positive attitude is not only desirable but also makes everyone's life easier.

Yet different threads come into play in the work environment that are not necessarily as pronounced in other settings. Your career is on the line, so there is an underlying sense of competition, self-preservation, and even ego at stake, as you and your coworkers strive for achievement, success, territory, stature, recognition, perks, and power. And, oh yes, did anyone mention money? A career is often at the core of a person's identity, so there is much to safeguard. But do we have to get ahead by acting so aggressively?

Some people fear being "too nice," because they don't want to appear too weak on the job, even though humility is a much-admired virtue, particularly in many world religions, as well as a respected leadership trait. Undoubtedly, this is tricky business. On one hand, you don't want your humility to allow professional colleagues to run you over. On the other, you need to stand up for yourself in order to succeed or not be overlooked.

Writing for the *Harvard Business Review*, John Baldoni refers to humility as an essential component of leadership because it "authenticates a person's humanity." In order to grow as a leader, we need to recognize both our strengths and our weaknesses, and having a healthy dose of humility is a vital part of that process. Baldoni suggests that in exercising humility, leaders need to "temper authority, look to promote others, and acknowledge what others do." Exemplifying this message, he quotes the late great University of Alabama football coach, Bear Bryant: "If anything goes bad, I did it. If anything goes semi-good, we did it. If anything goes really good, then you did it. That's all it takes to get people to win football games for you."

> Individual commitment to a group effort—that is what makes a team work, a company work, a society work, a civilization work.
>
> —VINCE LOMBARDI

Some people may consider civility in the workplace to be an incidental element within a package of soft skills—polite and courteous behavior that amounts to little and about which few care. In truth, it is one of the toughest and most advantageous weapons that any company can have in its arsenal. When it's part of a company culture, it acts as a "meta skill" that is both strategic and effective. Need I say that having a firm policy and a personal code of civility is the right thing to do?

50

Grow a Very Big Heart

Not to know is bad,
Not to want to know is worse,
Not to hope is unthinkable,
Not to care is unforgivable.

—IGBO NIGERIAN PROVERB

I truly believe compassion provides the basis of human
survival, the real value of human life, and without that
there is a basic piece missing.... We cannot be happy
ourselves without thinking about the happiness of others.

—THE DALAI LAMA

An older chimpanzee, attacked and defeated by another in a fight, slumps away. A third chimpanzee bystander, upon seeing his fellow primate in distress, comes over and puts his arm around the disheartened one in a show of consolation; the anguished screams of the injured chimpanzee cease. Empathetic occurrences like this and other instances of one animal rescuing or helping another—including one primate helping another get down from a tree—are commonly documented in the wild. Moreover, laboratory experiments have revealed that a captive chimpanzee that spends long, leisurely amounts of time grooming a fellow chimpanzee is likely to be rewarded by receiving a share of the groomed one's food, an act of reciprocity. Those two animal behaviors, according to renowned Emory University psychologist and primatologist Frans B. M. de Waal, demonstrate the "two pillars of human morality" as reflected in the golden rule—doing unto others (empathy) as you would like them to do unto you (reciprocity).

Charles Darwin, the first scientist to observe and question the origin of sympathy and compassion in the animal kingdom, determined that empathy, which precedes compassionate action, has been an important survival tool throughout the evolution of all members of the animal kingdom. Those who were more successful in this capacity were more likely to be sustained through their interactions with groups of the same species.

Compassion, and its importance in human life, is a central theme in all major world religions. In the Christian tradition, throughout the gospels, Jesus teaches that the poor, the afflicted, and the outcasts are all human beings deserving of our compassionate attention and action. Compassion for the suffering of all sentient beings is both the core and the central path of Buddhism, which teaches that we are all interconnected and interdependent.

> The problem of our time, of our century, is to achieve a global compassion; otherwise we run the risk that we will destroy ourselves.
>
> —PAUL EKMAN

Research scientists affiliated with the Center for Compassion and Altruism Research and Education at Stanford University (CCARE), among others, are currently exploring what stirs our compassion and why some people are more naturally disposed to be compassionate than others. The hope is that potential discoveries may reveal ways in which we can all become more compassionate, leading us to cultivate more prosocial behavior for the good of all society.

While empathy, compassion, and altruism are certainly linked, scientists do not necessarily agree on the exact definitions of these terms or the degree to which emotion is involved or not, which creates some confusion. Eminent psychologist and author Daniel Goleman uses the word *empathy* in three senses: "*knowing* another person's feelings; *feeling* what the person feels; and *responding compassionately* to another's distress." Although it is possible to recognize the emotion of others without having compassion, part and parcel of growing a very big heart encompasses both—seeing the suffering of others and feeling compelled to relieve it.

Loving-kindness, says the Dalai Lama, is primarily focused on wishing happiness for another person, whereas compassion is the wish to see another free of suffering. What is crucial is a sense of *connectedness*, "cultivating a state of mind that makes the sight of others' suffering unbearable to you. When others bleed, you bleed." Without cultivating this practice, you can have spontaneous flashes of compassion; however, they are not lasting. Cultivating compassion is a state of mind that promotes an automatic response to the suffering of others.

While suffering exists throughout the world, imbalances of natural resources, food, and energy threaten poorer nations to a larger degree than wealthier ones—disparities that beseech us to protect and nurture our global family. While Buddhists have always viewed the world as interconnected and interdependent, our economic and political realities have been slower to catch up to that way of thinking. Although our economic interdependence is now evident and openly acknowledged, the unfortunate rivalries between national political leaders, who focus on short-term interests and seek to dominate natural resources, often thwart our efforts to cultivate a "we" as opposed to an "all mine" mentality. This shortsighted vision may be sustainable for now but not over the long haul; it may, in fact, signal our end.

New York Times editorial columnist Bob Herbert points to the increasing inequality in the distribution of wealth in the United States in recent years, referring to the growing share of national income collected by the top 1 percent of wage earners. He cites statistics presented in the book *Aftershock*, written by Robert Reich, professor of public policy at the University of California, Berkeley, and former secretary of labor under President Bill Clinton. In the 1970s, the top 1 percent of wage earners garnered between 8 and 9 percent of the national income. In the 1980s, that group earned between 10 and 14 percent, and by the late 1990s their share of the national income soared to between 15 and 19 percent. The last year in which this data was compiled was 2007, when their share of the national income skyrocketed to more than 23 percent. Further, according to Reich, "the richest *one-tenth* of one percent, representing just 13,000 households, took in more than 11 percent of

> This country will not be a good place for any of us to live in unless we make it a good place for all of us to live in.
>
> —PRESIDENT THEODORE ROOSEVELT

total income" in 2007. The result of this astonishing disparity is that there is not enough spending power to go around among the population to sustain a flourishing economy.

Reich maintains that rising inequality is not only a result of structural economic changes but also the fault of policy makers who have failed to meet serious social and economic challenges. This has led to a breakdown of the social contract that dictates our "mutual commitments and responsibilities to one another." Empathy is required, he says, in order to determine what we owe one another in any community. With a diminishing middle class, the widening gulf between the rich and the poor reflects two different societies; it is difficult to determine whether declining empathy is the cause or the effect of that spread. Reich suggests that, while there is no magic bullet, policy changes could address such inequities. He says, however, that history has shown that "empathy is related to facing common challenges. The more people feel that they are in the same boat, the more they empathize with one another."

Other cultural factors may be causing shifts within our society as well. A 2010 study by the University of Michigan Institute for Social Research showed that there has been a 40 percent drop in empathy among college students from twenty to thirty years ago "as measured by standard tests of this personality trait." In a meta-analysis of seventy-two studies conducted between 1979 and 2009, researcher Sara Konrath and her associates, Edward O'Brien and Courtney Hsing, found that students today are less likely than those years ago to agree with statements such as "I sometimes try to understand my friends better by imagining how things look from their perspective" and "I often have tender, concerned feelings for people less fortunate than me."

> If you want others to be happy, practice compassion. If you want to be happy, practice compassion.
>
> —THE DALAI LAMA

In a separate but related analysis, Konrath, who is also affiliated with the University of Rochester Department of Psychiatry, found that representative samples of Americans viewed current college students—sometimes referred to as "generation me"—as "one of the most self-centered, narcissistic, competitive, confident and individualistic in recent history." While further research is required to determine the reasons for this decline in empathy, some have been advanced. Media exposure is one possibility. A growing body of research, for instance, is pointing to the effect of violent media in video games, which may numb people to others' pain. The hyper-competitive atmosphere of celebrity-driven reality shows goes against the grain of slowing down, listening, and offering sympathy to someone who may need it. Another conjecture is that our computer-age society may contribute to the ability to establish friendships online and tune out when you don't need them, which may affect offline behavior. According to O'Brien, "College students today may be so busy worrying about themselves and their own issues that they don't have time to spend empathizing with others, or at least perceive such time to be limited."

Although Daniel Goleman argues that "our brain has been preset for kindness," he also says that "self-absorption in all its forms kills empathy, let alone compassion." We empathize more strongly when we focus on another and establish an emotional connection. When we focus on ourselves, our mind contracts as we think about the rest of the world. When we focus on others, our world expands. "Simply paying attention allows us to build an emotional connection," says Goleman. "Lacking attention, empathy hasn't a chance." Further, Goleman cites Stephanie Preston and Frans de Waal, who note, "In today's era of e-mail, commuting, frequent moves, and bedroom communities, the scales are increasingly tipped against the automatic and accurate perception of others' emotional state, without which empathy is impossible."

Author, photographer, and Buddhist monk Matthieu Ricard says, "A more altruistic society is the answer to our times," with less greed and more consideration for others, wishing them to flourish. Our own suffering, he says, allows us to see that suffering is not desirable, which is why we need to think of others as well, and not remain in our own small bubbles. Reaching a state of total compassion changes the way you act, he says, "because how you act is the reflection of your worldview." We must consider the legacy that we are offering future generations. As Paul Ekman suggests, if we cannot bring ourselves to be compassionate for the children of Darfur, perhaps we can at least feel compassionate for our own children and grandchildren, and the world we are creating for them.

~~~ 51 ~~~

Reel in
What's Real

Be your authentic self. Your authentic self is who
you are when you have no fear of judgment, or
before the world starts pushing you around and
telling you who you're supposed to be. Your
fictional self is who you are when you have a social
mask on to please everyone else. Give yourself
permission to be your authentic self.

—DR. PHIL

Let me tell you a story ... you happen to be the main character. You're
at a party with guests you've never met. Some are in fancy clothes and
expensive jewelry, others in jeans and crumpled shirts; a few are sleekly
dressed, all in black, while another sector sports tweed and corduroy. They
hail from Wall Street, Main Street, college towns, and rural roads. As you
eavesdrop and observe their behavior, some of the crowd appears sophis-
ticated and polished, while you note a more down-to-earth simplicity in
others. You hear conversations that are glib, sometimes posturing or
haughty, while others sound sincere and inviting. There are pockets of roar-
ing laughter while others smile thinly. These guests range from the preten-
tious and pompous to real class acts. Now you get to pick who you want
to talk to. How do *you* act? As you circle the room, are you the same with
every person whom you meet, or do you become the person you think
they expect you to be? Do you find yourself trying too hard to impress
some of the guests—with your accomplishments, knowledge, possessions,
or repartee? Are there people beneath your notice? With whom do you feel

comfortable—or not? At the end of the evening, does anyone get to know the *real* you, or do you hide that person, from them and from yourself?

You can probably see where I'm going with all of this. That party, however, isn't just for one night; it happens over a lifetime. Becoming authentic, deeply genuine, is something we do over the course of our lives as we wrestle with our insecurities and the challenges of our journey, high and low. We often feel that we have to be someone else in order to be liked and respected. It doesn't feel very good to have to act like a phony, put on a front, or hide behind something we are not, but we do it anyway, out of our deep need to be liked and to belong. No doubt you met some people at that party in whom you spotted that same phony behavior, but also recall that you neither liked nor connected with them. You immediately cast aside those who were know-it-alls, or who grabbed the spotlight, in part because you couldn't get a word in edgewise or have an opinion that counted. You also felt icky around those who were needlessly disparaging or supercilious, because they made you feel as though you didn't belong. Hopefully, however, you connected with some folks who were the real deal, the genuine article, people you liked and who liked you back. You could be exactly who you are, which made you want to party on forever.

The message here is very simple: Don't try to show off or be something you're not. You'll be miserable and so will the people around you. Just be yourself and do what you enjoy doing. You are what you are. Be serious, but don't take yourself too seriously. That doesn't mean that you don't grow, learn, improve, or evolve; just do those things in a real way. Find your center, find your way home, to the authentic you, the real deal. And when you find others who think and act like you, hold them close and hang on tight!

Plant a Seed

To laugh often and much; to win the respect of
intelligent people and the affection of children ... to
leave the world a better place ... to know even one
life has breathed easier because you have lived.
This is to have succeeded.

—RALPH WALDO EMERSON

In the movie *It's a Wonderful Life*, the protagonist, George Bailey, has an opportunity—with a little help from an angel—to see what the world would be like had he not lived. He comes to discover how his life has made a difference in the lives of others. Unlike George Bailey, we do not have the gift of this vision; nonetheless, we can create our path through our best positive intentions and actions.

Most of us want to do something in our lives that is meaningful, and we each pursue that goal differently, as determined by our intentions, circumstances, and gifts. While some of us have big dreams about what we hope to achieve, most of our accomplishments will be measured in the small steps and ordinary actions of our everyday lives. What can make the biggest difference and provide us with life's greatest rewards are the strength of our character and the relationships that we foster with those around us. Our connections with family members, friends, colleagues, and other associates, and our cultivation of those relationships, provide deeper meaning in our lives, as well as a sense of purpose.

The strength of your relationships will develop, in large part, according to how well you treat the

If you want to work
for world peace, go
home and love
your families.

—MOTHER TERESA

people in your life, and everything that you do counts. You may be the head of a large corporation that produces a hefty bottom line; if you behave like a jerk, however, decimating the morale of your employees, what does that say about you? You may sit in the front pew of church every Sunday and even tithe, but if your mind is corrupted by prejudice and bigotry, making you intolerant of others, what is the value of a closed heart full of hatred? You may perform self-aggrandizing acts for an organization or the community for the benefit of many; however, if at home you are abusive to your spouse and children, what matters more? In the presence of those you know, your behavior may be upstanding and impeccable, but do you act the same way when shielded by a cloak of anonymity?

There is no road map in life, and no single act defines us. Few of us will become great leaders or inventers, discover cures for diseases, or otherwise alter the scope and destiny of humankind. However, when we raise our children with compassion, are kind to strangers, offer a sympathetic ear, extend a helping hand, and do the right thing, these are contributions of which we are all capable. These are actions that directly affect the lives of those around us and make a difference, whether in small or large ways. These are seeds we each can plant.

> The purpose of life is to contribute in some way to making things better.
>
> —ROBERT F. KENNEDY

Regardless of our other accomplishments and deeds, the legacy that we will each leave behind will be shaped by our character, thoughts, attitudes, and conduct, reflected in the manner in which we respect, treat, and value all people. Every person on this earth who lives and breathes will bequeath this legacy and, in this regard, we each have the power to be extraordinary.

What you believe and value; your behavior; your relationships; what you say; how you develop and use your talents, passions, and ideas; what you choose as your life's work; and what you give of yourself—these comprise who you are, imprinting your own life and the lives of those you touch. In sum, the expression and implementation of all these sectors shape your unique contribution to the world and humanity. As you explore ways to imbue your life with a sense of purpose that serves humankind, there are additional strategies you may consider.

Find something you're passionate about and keep
tremendously interested in it.

—JULIA CHILD

Discovering your passion and applying it to your life's work—whether it is
paid or volunteer, a career or raising a family, or even pursuing a hobby—raise
the likelihood of increasing your enjoyment. Dr. Mihaly Csikszentmihalyi,
director of the Quality of Life Research Center at Claremont Graduate
University and cofounder of the discipline of positive psychology, is most
noted for his seminal work *Flow: The Psychology of Optimal Experience*. Human
beings are said to be in a state of flow when they are so involved in their
present task and work that they lose sight of the hands on the clock.
Discovering your strengths and talents may point you in this direction as
you optimize what you do best. *StrengthsFinder 2.0* is both a book and an
online test that can be taken and scored, providing feedback on your five
most important strengths. In addition, it may be helpful to take a free
online test at www.authentichappiness.com to reveal the five areas of your
life that give you the greatest happiness.

Some people dream of success ... while others wake up and
work hard at it.

—ANONYMOUS

Be good at what you do, but know that much of any success is attributed to
hard work. It is important to establish goals for yourself. In *The How of Happiness*,
author and psychologist Sonja Lyubomirsky lists setting goals as one of twelve
strategies that can help each one of us achieve greater happiness. "People who
strive for something personally significant ... are far happier than those who
don't have strong dreams or aspirations," says Dr. Lyubomirsky. She also
writes about finding *flow*, mentioned above, as one of the twelve strategies.
Further, University of North Carolina psychologist Barbara Fredrickson iden-
tifies taking pride in your accomplishments as a positive emotion, because it
can serve as a motivator that helps you do your best work.

Someone's sitting in the shade today because someone planted a tree a long time ago.
—WARREN BUFFETT

Work, inspired by a vision for the future, can benefit humankind, whether it is the building of a playground in a local park that you spearhead, your participation in the green movement, or teaching a group of underprivileged citizens how to grow gardens or develop small businesses so that they can sustain their own lives. In this regard, there are forests of trees that have yet to be planted.

"We've always done it this way" is not necessarily a good thing.
—REAR ADMIRAL GRACE MURRAY HOPPER

Think creatively, whether you're inventing a product, brainstorming ideas for a charity fundraiser, or finding different ways to teach students. I once had the pleasure of meeting "Amazing Grace," quoted above, who was known for her multiplicity of accomplishments in the field of computer programming. As her own visual reminder of how everything does not always have to be the same, Hopper had a clock mounted on the wall with hands that moved counterclockwise!

Thou shalt not be a victim. Thou shalt not be a perpetrator. Above all, thou shalt not be a bystander.
—UNITED STATES HOLOCAUST MEMORIAL MUSEUM

Recognize the difference between right and wrong and have the courage and strength of your moral convictions to stand up, speak out, and act.

I do not want to die ... until I have faithfully made the most of my talent and cultivated the seed that was placed in me until the last small twig has grown.

—KÄTHE KOLLWITZ

Know your value and recognize that you are a unique human being capable of making a difference in this world. Be bold and courageous in your journey, taking small steps that enable you to climb mountains and traverse valleys, and also chart a path for others.

A Call to Action

Plea for a Polite Planet

> There can be hope only for a society which acts as
> one big family, not as many separate ones.
>
> —ANWAR SADAT

As a passenger on a city bus in Washington, D.C., a close friend of mine witnessed and relayed to me the following episode, which occurred one warm midafternoon in late summer. On a route from Georgetown to the busy city center, people got on and off the bus. At one stop, a tiny, elegant, but frail elderly woman with a walker excitedly boarded the public transport. She was on her way, the woman told the driver, to McDonald's, where she planned to get a delicious fruit smoothie. Seated in the handicapped area near the driver, she continued to chatter about how much she was looking forward to the smoothie as well as which flavor she was going to order. As the bus turned onto 13th Street, however, the multiple lanes were teeming with traffic; double-parked cars only added to the congestion. The regular stop for the bus, the one closest to McDonald's, was more than a block away and across the busy street, requiring strenuous effort for an older person to negotiate. Aware of the difficulty that his elderly passenger might face, the bus driver suddenly went rogue and totally veered off his route; the woman expressed alarm, no longer sure where she was headed. Reassuring her, all the while patiently weaving a circuitous path in and out of one-way streets, the driver, after some minutes, pulled up directly in front of the door of the fast-food chain. After helping his frail but relieved passenger off the bus, he reclaimed his seat behind the wheel. The remaining passengers on the bus, including my friend, broke out into spontaneous applause.

This is an inspiring example of how a deliberate gesture of kindness can make a difference in someone else's life; it is also an illustration of how we can live in community together. In order for this act to occur, first the bus driver had to *pay attention* to and notice his elderly rider. Second, he had to empathize with her condition; her frailty had to resonate with him. Third, he had to be guided by compassion, allowing his heart to go out to her and impelling him to do something positive that would ostensibly relieve the passenger from further anxiety, suffering, and harm. Fourth, he had to be willing to take a risk and make an effort. In a hectic city known for its colossal traffic jams and high levels of stress, this ordinary bus driver went out of his way to offer uncommon assistance, to a stranger no less. It was a deliberate act, but perhaps even a heroic one: In a split-second decision, the driver made a sacrifice, risking recrimination and complaints from other passengers, which could have resulted in a serious rebuke from his employer, potentially costing him his job. A detail not to be dismissed, by the way, is that the driver and the elderly woman were not of the same race.

> The greatest dilemma in life is to fail to do something little that you could do because you were waiting to do something heroic you couldn't do. Think small and get the job done, beginning with yourself.
>
> —LORD CHESTERFIELD

Compare this deliberate act of loving-kindness to intentional acts of cruelty, sometimes shielded by anonymity, where people physically abuse, bully, and otherwise harm fellow human beings. Think, also, of those of us who fall somewhere in the middle, as we *fail to notice* someone in need, or if we do see, instead seek distance, doing nothing to lend a hand. Stanford University professor emeritus of psychology Philip Zimbardo, whose "Heroic Imagination Project" I referred to earlier ("Choose Your Heroes Wisely"), separates the population into three groups. Only a small percentage of the population, he says, commits truly evil acts, while another small percentage at the opposite end of the spectrum performs extraordinary ones; at issue is the large percentage of people in the middle whose inertia compels them to do little or nothing. Zimbardo contends that we can create change, in part, by galvanizing this "middle sector" into action, encouraging ordinary citizens to increase their involvement by inspiring them to make a difference in their communities.

We have explored ways that you, as an individual, can help bring about a shift toward a more civilized society and a polite planet, based on the manner in which you interact with others, treating them with respect and consideration. Through your conscious positive behavior—which *you* control—you have the power to effect constructive change in the world,

> When you pray,
> move your feet.
>
> —AFRICAN PROVERB

beginning with yourself and the example that you set. Every day you can turn your genuinely good intentions into inspiring actions that make a difference and foster a better world. Yes, that might take a little effort. There may be times when you have to take a risk. Having a conscience and a high moral code are absolutely essential. And, undoubtedly, you have to believe and have a little faith. Those are the first steps toward change.

Do you want to see behavior on the planet improve? If so, what are you willing to do about it? Transformation into a more civilized society begins right here, at the grassroots level, with your efforts and mine. Stepping up to the plate and doing your part every day provides traction so the wheels of change can turn. There is, however, another very important step. Get others to join you. Become a *leader*. As marketing guru and author Seth Godin might put it, form a tribe. Stand up for respectful behavior. Motivate others to do the same thing. Speak out against any form of incivility and indignity. Encourage people within groups to think and act the way you do. Giant leaps and strides have come as a result of one person's courage, drive, and willingness to stick his or her neck out. Before you protest, "Oh no, I'm not really a leader" or "I don't really belong to a lot of clubs and organizations" or "I'm not particularly persuasive or influential" or "I'm much too shy," it's time to rethink.

Consider this true story about what a small gesture of activism accomplished. On the first day of school in 2007, in a small town in Nova Scotia, Canada, a ninth-grade boy wore a pink polo shirt to class, where he was humiliated by a group of bullies who called him a homosexual and threatened to beat him up. Fortunately, two twelfth-grade boys decided that enough was enough. Going to a nearby discount store, the two seniors bought fifty pink shirts, including tank tops, to be worn the next day. That night they e-mailed all their classmates to spread the word in support of a campaign they dubbed a "sea of pink." As a result, literally hundreds of students came to school the following day wearing pink. Not only were the bullies silenced, but also the taunted ninth-grade boy was able to hold his head high. As one of the two organizers said to CBC News afterward, "If you can get more people against them ... to show that we're not going to put up with it and support each other, then they're not as big a group as they think they are." Not a bad outcome for a day's work by two young men.

Your efforts to embrace and promote civilized behavior may be less public. A perfect place to begin is within your family, finding ways to build respectful, rather than acrimonious, relationships. If you have children, there is a strong possibility that they will be influenced by your behavior and pass along your parenting style to the next generation. Paying attention to your children's behavior and teaching them to be respectful and accepting of others may well be one of your most important legacies. The same holds true for any position you hold in which young minds are under your watch, whether you are a teacher, a Girl or Boy Scout leader, a pediatrician, a clergy member, a coach, a bus driver, or the head of a community center.

You may be the president of a corporation or own a small business. Establishing a culture that incorporates a zero-tolerance policy for incivility and rewards cooperative efforts, and then hiring employees who fit into that culture, is one way to ensure civil behavior and an environment where employees feel safe and productive. Monitor the behavior of your managers and employees, coaching them away from any abuse. Honoring and valuing customers and clients as part of your business model is yet another way you can extend the circle of respect and trust.

Perhaps you are the leader of an organization. In that position, you may be able to steer a group discussion so that it doesn't veer off topic and wander into the realm of personal attack and abuse. Even if you are not the designated leader, you can become one by choosing to withdraw your support for discussions or behavior that is destructive.

Civility initiatives are springing up all over the country, on college campuses, as mission-driven independent organizations and associations, and within school systems. Some are national endeavors and others are local. Check them out. This may well be your time to jump in, show support, and spread the word.

Much of the discussion on incivility today focuses on the current political climate, particularly in the United States. Unfortunately, those responsible for the uncivil behavior generally have the loudest voices, and use those voices to shout others down. I do not object to lively political discussion among individuals or groups who hold strong opposing points of view. Having an open forum for discussion is vital for the democratic process. However, I do object to inflammatory free-for-all discourse, with no-holds-barred exchanges, intended to incite crowds rather than inform them and build consensus. Often, such tactics serve as red herrings—bait swallowed by opponents and the public, diverting everyone's focus from engaging in meaningful discussions of the issues and forging solutions to those issues. Leaders and candidates do a disservice to the public by behaving in this manner; the public, in turn, compounds that disservice by giving credence to that sort of posturing. Compromise and consensus building are essential so that decisions can be reached; otherwise, nothing ever gets accomplished. I also find fault with ego-driven personalities and those with narrow, short-sighted vision, who are more concerned with enhancing their own personal power than with promoting the overall good of society.

> The most practical kind of politics is the politics of decency.
>
> —PRESIDENT THEODORE ROOSEVELT

We do not always agree, nor should we. However, we have very serious and urgent problems to solve in this country and around the world. We will never be able to solve them if we all think we are right and, thus, are unwilling to genuinely listen and understand a point of view other than our own. Undoubtedly, respect engenders increased cooperation; so do civil ears and tongues. Civility is not the only answer to our problems. However, it does create an opportunity for *civil dialogue*, a platform for exploring solutions to our problems. Without that, I guarantee that nothing will happen.

We also need to understand that all people do not think the same way. A citizen from Shanghai, China, will have an entirely different perspective on the world than one from Sioux City, Iowa; each of us has our own context that shapes the way we think. (For those who may want to explore why liberals and conservatives in the United States think differently, I strongly urge you to study the research of University of Virginia social psychologist Jonathan Haidt and his colleagues, much of which is available online.) Further, neuroscientists are beginning to explore the possibilities that the neural circuitry of our brains may have dissimilarities, which may cause some groups of people to think and react differently than others.

Regardless of our divergence in ideology and outlook, it is imperative that we find a way to cooperate, locally and globally. Although, historically, cooperation has always been easier to foster in smaller enclaves, in our world today even smaller communities are becoming less homogeneous. *Globalization* is a term that becomes relevant in our own neighborhoods, as we live, work, and play alongside people of different cultures. This often arouses our fears and suspicions, if not prejudice and bigotry. Therefore, we must learn to work together and coexist for the common good of all humankind, because it is the moral thing to do, the right thing to do.

> My humanity is bound up in yours, for we can only be human together.
>
> —ARCHBISHOP DESMOND TUTU

In this book I have purposely refrained from expressing my personal political or religious views. My plea, however, is that, as human beings, we grow very big and compassionate hearts, and embrace a spiritual belief in our shared humanity.

Human beings are social animals, and we need one another in order to survive. *Ubuntu* is an African word that, while difficult to translate, is one whose meaning we should each know. I have heard it described as "I in you, you in me." Archbishop Desmond Tutu translates *ubuntu* as "I cannot be, without you." He explains further, "When we want to give high praise to someone we say, 'Hey, so-and-so has *ubuntu*.' Then you are generous, you are hospitable, you are friendly and caring and compassionate. You share what you have. A person with *ubuntu* is open and available to others, affirming of others, does not feel threatened that others are able and good, for he or she has a proper self-assurance that comes from knowing that he or she belongs in a greater whole.... A person is a person through other persons."

I myself have no words more eloquent than *ubuntu*.

None of us is perfect, nor will we ever be. What we can do, however, is *improve* our behavior toward one another on a daily basis. There is also something to be said for a collective effort, where our positive intentions and actions mirror one another's. World War II was not won by the singular efforts of a few people; the Allies were victorious, in large part, because *collectively* we joined hands and made sacrifices for a common goal, which we believed served the common good, from regions of combat to victory gardens.

I cannot say whether things will get better if we change; what I can say is that they must change if they are to get better.

—GEORG C. LICHTENBERG

Once, when black abolitionist and women's rights activist Sojourner Truth was giving an anti-slavery speech, she was heckled by a man in the audience. "Old woman, do you think that your talk about slavery does any good? Why, I don't care any more for your talk than I do for the bite of a flea." "Perhaps not," she replied, "but the Lord willing, I'll keep you scratching." My hope is that this book will keep *you* scratching.

By opening our eyes, minds, and hearts, and treating each other with respect and consideration, we can achieve greater awareness, understanding, and, ultimately, acceptance of one another. I end this plea by asking that we join together, with hope, vision, and commitment to saving civility, creating a polite planet—a better world in which we all can live and thrive.

✍ ACKNOWLEDGMENTS

I have always been envious of authors who are able to produce very good books in what seems, to me, a relatively short period of time; that, however, was not my process. Passionate about my topic, I dreamed of writing this book for many years, and it took almost two to actually complete it, with the help of a lot of people. Without question, I would not have been able to accomplish that feat without the support, patience, and understanding of my loving family—husband, Tom, and daughter, Katie—to whom I dedicate this publication. Early on, they learned to look to each other when any one of us asked, "What's for dinner?" and to take up the mantle and carry on because "Mom has a deadline." Whether reading countless drafts of chapters, providing feedback on which ideas made sense, or encouraging me with a "you can do it" boost when I needed it most, their unflagging belief in me never wavered. I appreciate and love you both hugely; you mean the world to me.

I also want to honor the memory of my identical-twin mothers who shared me as their only child. It was my birth mother, Maxine, who certified me in etiquette from the cradle, and my aunt, Madaline, who always kept me in line but taught me what unconditional love meant. They would have loved seeing "their" daughter in print.

Recognizing in the early stages that I would write a better book if I had professional guidance, I was fortunate to meet Coleen O'Shea, of the Allen O'Shea Literary Agency, who put me in touch with editor par excellence Meredith Peters Hale, whose help with the editorial content was immeasurable. It was Meredith who not only prodded me to substantiate my ideas with statistics and further research, she sometimes gently muzzled me when my words were a little too bossy or too heavily tinged with a wagging finger. I am also grateful to Meredith for introducing me to my copyeditor, Diana Drew, who showed me that my writing would be much friendlier to readers if I addressed them directly in the second person as opposed to the third. I am further indebted to Diana for her confidence in my work, which led her to introduce it to the folks at SkyLight Paths Publishing on my behalf. Frankly, I cannot imagine being with a more professional, intelligent, supportive, and collaborative group of people than those at SkyLight Paths. I appreciate each of their talents and contributions. In particular, however, I am thankful to Emily Wichland, vice president of editorial and production, who has shown great belief in my message and support for my project; and to Stuart M. Matlins, publisher, who graciously considered this book by a first-time author.

There are a number of friends and acquaintances who deserve kudos, as they spent many hours reading my unedited manuscript and offering constructive comments. Dr. James Corry put his own PhD to work as he helped me sift through and make sense of the research of fellow social scientists. Fredric George, a friend since childhood, let me know when "my voice" was evident or absent, mentioning a time or two when my declarations went a bit overboard! Two nationally recognized individuals, Sybil Steinberg, former *Publishers Weekly* Forecasts editor, and Frank Deford, author and NPR contributor, reviewed my manuscript and subsequently agreed to write endorsements before I had secured a publisher; thank you, Sybil and Frank. Additionally, I appreciate all individuals who read my work and wrote favorable comments. Further, I am forever grateful for my minister, Reverend John Branson, of Christ and Holy Trinity Episcopal Church, who not only took time out of his overly burdened schedule to review my manuscript, but who taught our congregation about what it means to live in community together.

Sometimes needing help with locating research to support my ideas, I reached out to Tony Bingham, president of the National American Society for Training and Development, and to Lee Rainie, director of the Pew Research Center's Internet and American Life Project. Neither of them knew who I was but responded within minutes with sources from which I gleaned the information I needed. Thank you, gentlemen.

I am appreciative of a circle of close friends who, during social occasions, supported me in my endeavor by patiently listening and nodding as I chirped on ad nauseam about my subject matter, when, in fact, they likely wanted to roll their eyes or smack me!

Lastly, I am grateful to each person who reads *Saving Civility*. I have faith that people can alter their respective behavior with others for the better. Having learned a great deal from researching and writing this book, I myself have changed and improved upon my own faults in a number of ways. Civility is a communal language with which we all can resonate. My hope is that we all will share a vision and make every effort going forward to be uncommonly respectful, considerate, and accepting of each other, saving civility for all of society.

❧ NOTES

Introduction: The Rise of Rude, Crude, and Attitude— How We're All Part of the Problem

Christakis and Fowler 2009.
"Aggravating Circumstances": Farkas et al. 2002.
AP–Ipsos: *USA Today* 2005.
ABC poll: Cohen and Langer 2006.
Gallup 2009.
Rasmussen Reports 2009.
Weber Shandwick 2011.
Background on history of civility and etiquette: Kasson 1990, Caldwell 1999.
Gilbert 2009.
Technorati/blogosphere: Winn 2008.
User-generated web content: Modus Associates 2010.
Pew Research Center/Internet use: Rainie 2010.
Social media: Nielsen Wire 2010.
Radicati Group 2009.
E-mail/*Wall Street Journal*: Vascellaro 2009.
E-mail statistics: Radicati and Khmartseva 2009.
Radicati Group 2009.
CTIA 2010.
Pew Research Center/teen cell phones: Lenhart et al. 2010.
Carter 1998.
Zimbardo: Center for Compassion and Altruism Research and Education 2010, "Meng Wu Lecture Series Presents: Phil Zimbardo."
School superintendent: Purdy 2001.
Guinness 2008.
New York Times/polarization: Posner 2005.
Iyengar and Hahn 2007.
Pearson and Porath 2009.
Sutton 2007.
Blackshaw 2008.
Simon 2005.

Gladwell 2005.
Baker and O'Malley 2008.
Society for Human Resource Management study: Burke 2004.
PricewaterhouseCoopers 2009.
Background on generation Y: Tapscott 2008.

3 Smile

Goleman 2006.
Keltner 2009.
Ekman 2003.
Helson: Keltner 2009.
Stibich: Zhivotovskaya 2008.
Pease and Pease 2006.

4 See Yourself as Others See You

Background on body language: Pease and Pease 2006.
Goleman 2006.
Mehrabian: Pease and Pease 2006.

5 Sharpen Your Social Antenna

Ekman research: Keltner 2009.
Background on social interaction: Goleman 2006.
Pease and Pease 2006.

6 Respect the Boundaries of Others

Edward T. Hall: Straker 2010.
Givens: Rosenbloom 2006.
Morrison and Conway 2004.

7 Listen Up

Kashdan 2009.

8 Discern the Right Meaning

Difficult Conversations: Stone, Patton, and Heen 1999.

10 Recognize the Power of Words

Background on verbal gaffes: Zaslow 2010.
Kaslow: Zaslow 2010.
Servcorp 2009.

11 Hold Your Tongue

Forni 2002.
Allegheny Center for Political Participation 2010.

12 Resist Rhetoric

Harvard Business School newsletter: Hanna 2010.

13 Disagree Agreeably

Difficult Conversations: Stone, Patton, and Heen 1999.

14 Keep a Negotiation on Track

Fisher and Ury 1981.

17 Build Trust

Kosfeld 2010.

18 Strive for Truth

Ericsson 2004.

19 Take the High Road

Maxwell 2004.

20 Laugh at Least Once a Day

Tierney 2007.
Provine 2000.
Background on laughter research: Johnson 2007.
Scott: Thompson 2006.
Kent and Liverpool study/altruism: Medical News 2007.
Cousins 1979.
Berk and Tan, body's response to laughter: *ScienceDaily* 2010.

21 Just Be Nice!

Kaplan Thaler and Koval 2006.

22 Cultivate Optimism

Fredrickson 2009.
Background on benefits of optimism: Seligman 1998.
Background on authentic happiness research: Seligman 2002.

23 Embrace Kindness

Lyubomirsky 2008.

24 Live Generously

University of Notre Dame 2009.
Post and Neimark 2007.
Kristof 2010.
Background on how giving can make you happy: Tierney 2008.
Brown: Tierney 2008.
Background on how giving can make you happy: Williams 2007.
Oxytocin and building trust: Zak 2008.
Oxytocin and generosity: Zak 2009.

25 Practice Gratitude

Moss 2007.
Emmons 2008.
Lyubomirsky 2008.
Tsang: Post and Neimark 2007.

26 Embody Enough

Vonnegut 2005.
Lea and Webley: *PsyBlog* 2008.
Vohs, Mead, and Goode 2008.
Gilbert: Lyubomirsky 2008.
Background on hedonic treadmill: Lyubomirsky 2008.
Harvard study of faculty: Brooks 2008.
Dunn and Norton: Bennett 2009.
Van Boven and Gilovich: Bennett 2009.
World Values Survey: University of Michigan Institute for Social Research 2008.
University of Michigan, University of Leicester, and Erasmus University studies: Weir and Johnson 2007.
Background on Danish society: Weir and Johnson 2007, Vogel 2008.
Kaare Christensen: CBS News 2008.
University of Cambridge study: Weir and Johnson 2007.
Winfrey 2009.
Ben-Shahar: CBS News 2008.

27 Adapt Adeptly

Sony presentation: Fisch, McLeod, and Brenman 2008.
Fredrickson 2009.

29 Drive Gently on the Road

University of Utah: Watson and Strayer 2010.
Pew Internet and American Life Project: Madden and Rainie 2010.
AAA Foundation for Traffic Safety: Mizell 1995.

31 Remember What Your Mother Taught You

"The Smell of Virtue": Liljenquist, Zhong, and Galinsky 2010.

32 Teach Your Children Well

Klass 2009.
Howard: Klass 2009.
University of Illinois at Urbana-Champaign 2008.
Reuters 2010.
Linn: Thomas 2009.

34 Mind Your Cybermanners

Pew Research Center: Anderson and Rainie 2010.
Weber Shandwick 2010.
Intel 2009.

35 Time It Right

Emmons 2008.

37 Dress to Fit

Newsweek poll: Bennett 2010.
Deborah Rhode: Bennett 2010.

38 Apologize

Lazare 2004.
Robbennolt 2010.
Tavris and Aronson 2007.
Festinger: Tavris and Aronson 2007.
Gover: Tavris and Aronson 2007.

39 Learn to Forgive

Etty Hillesum: Hoffman 1996.
West Nickel Mines School: Dean 2006.
Lyubomirsky 2008.
Fourteen hundred scientific studies: Post and Neimark 2007.
Enright 2001.

40 Celebrate Diversity

Peace It Together: www.peaceittogether.com.

42 Consider Your Fellow Travelers

Travelocity 2009.

47 Choose Your Heroes Wisely

Franco and Zimbardo 2010.

48 Enhance Your Likeability

Sanders 2005.

49 Work at Workplace Civility

Pearson and Porath 2009.
Meyer 2006.
Baldoni 2009.

50 Grow a Very Big Heart

De Waal 2010.
Darwin 2003.
Center for Compassion and Altruism Research and Education 2010, "About Us."
Goleman 2006.
Dalai Lama and Ekman 2009.
Herbert 2010.
Robert Reich interview: Marsh 2010.
Empathy: University of Michigan Institute for Social Research 2010.
Ricard: Center for Compassion and Altruism Research and Education 2010,
    "Interview with Matthieu Ricard."

52 Plant a Seed

Csikszentmihalyi 1990.
Lyubomirsky 2008.
Fredrickson 2009.

A Call to Action: Plea for a Polite Planet

Zimbardo: Center for Compassion and Altruism Research and Education 2010,
    "Meng Wu Lecture Series Presents: Phil Zimbardo."
Godin 2008.
CBC News 2007.
Tutu 1999.

✍ REFERENCES

Allegheny College Center for Political Participation. 2010. "10 Tips to Improve Civility" (20 May). http://sites.allegheny.edu/civilityaward/research/college-democrats-and-republicans-release-joint-statement-"ten-tips-to-improve-civility" (accessed May 24, 2010).

Anderson, Janna Q., and Lee Rainie. 2010. "The Future of Social Relations." Report: Pew Research Center (2 July). www.pewinternet.org/~/media/Files/Reports/2010/PIP_Future_of_Internet_%202010_social_relations.pdf (accessed Aug. 9, 2010).

Baker, William F., and Michael O'Malley. 2008. *Leading with Kindness: How Good People Consistently Get Superior Results.* New York: AMACOM.

Baldoni, John. 2009. "Humility as a Leadership Trait." *Harvard Business Review.* Weblog post (15 Sept.). http://blogs.hbr.org/baldoni/2009/09/humility_as_a_leadership_trait.html (accessed Aug. 8, 2010).

Bennett, Drake. 2009. "Happiness: A Buyer's Guide. Money Can Improve Your Life, But Not in the Ways You Think." *The Boston Globe* (23 Aug.).

Bennett, Jessica. 2010. "The Beauty Advantage: How Looks Affect Your Work, Your Career, Your Life." *Newsweek* (19 July).

Blackshaw, Pete. 2008. *Satisfied Customers Tell Three Friends, Angry Customers Tell 3,000: Running a Business in Today's Consumer-Driven World.* New York: Crown Business.

Brooks, Arthur C. 2008. "Does Money Make You Happy?" *Christian Science Monitor* (24 June).

Burke, Mary. 2004. *Generational Differences Survey Report.* Report: Society for Human Resource Management (August). www.shrm.org/Research/SurveyFindings/Documents/Generational%20Differences%20Survey%20Report.pdf (accessed July 12, 2009).

Caldwell, Mark. 1999. *A Short History of Rudeness: Manners, Morals, and Misbehavior in Modern America.* New York: Picador.

Carter, Stephen L. 1998. *Civility: Manners, Morals, and the Etiquette of Democracy.* New York: Basic Books.

CBC News. 2007. "Bullied Student Tickled Pink by Schoolmates' T-shirt Campaign" (19 Sept.). www.cbc.ca/canada/nova-scotia/story/2007/09/18/pink-tshirts-students.html (accessed Sept. 11, 2010).

CBS News. 2008. "And the Happiest Place on Earth Is ..." (12 June). *60 Minutes.* www.cbsnews.com/stories/2008/02/14/60minutes/main3833797.shtml (accessed May 16, 2010).

Center for Compassion and Altruism Research and Education. 2010. "About Us." http://ccare.stanford.edu/aboutus/center-compassion-and-altruism-research-and-education (accessed June 7, 2011).

———. 2010. "Interview with Matthieu Ricard." Video. http://ccare.stanford.edu/content/interview-matthieu-ricard (accessed May 9, 2011).

———. 2010. "Meng Wu Lecture Series Presents: Phil Zimbardo." Video of a lecture by Philip Zimbardo, "The Lucifer Effect in Action: My Journey from Evil to Heroism," at Stanford University, Palo Alto, CA (14 Jan.). http://ccare.stanford.edu/content/ meng-wu-lecture-series-presents-phil-zimbardo (accessed May 9, 2011).

Christakis, Nicholas A., and James H. Fowler. 2009. *Connected: The Surprising Power of Our Social Networks and How They Shape Our Lives.* New York: Little, Brown.

Cohen, Jon, and Gary Langer. 2006. "Poll: Rudeness in America." ABC News. http://abcnews.go.com/2020/US/story?id=1574155 (accessed Feb. 2010).

Cousins, Norman. 1979. *Anatomy of an Illness as Perceived by the Patient.* New York: W. W. Norton.

Csikszentmihalyi, Mihaly. 1990. *Flow: The Psychology of Optimal Experience.* New York: Harper & Row.

CTIA. 2010. "U.S. Wireless Quick Facts." CTIA–The Wireless Association (June). www.ctia.org/advocacy/research/index.cfm/aid/10323 (accessed Aug. 5, 2010).

Dalai Lama and Paul Ekman. 2009. *Emotional Awareness: Overcoming the Obstacles to Psychological Balance and Compassion—A Conversation between the Dalai Lama and Paul Ekman.* New York: Times/Henry Holt.

Darwin, Charles. 2003. *The Expression of Emotion in Man and Animals.* Boston: Indypublish.

Dean, Jamie. 2006. "Paradise Lost." *WORLD Magazine* (14 Oct.). www.worldmag.com/articles/12298 (accessed July 17, 2010).

De Waal, Frans B. M. 2010. "The Evolution of Empathy." In *The Compassionate Instinct: The Science of Human Goodness*. Edited by Dacher Keltner, Jason Marsh, and Jeremy Adam Smith. New York: W. W. Norton.

Ekman, Paul. 2003. *Emotions Revealed: Recognizing Faces and Feelings to Improve Communication and Emotional Life*. New York: Times Books.

Emmons, Robert A. 2008. *Thanks! How Practicing Gratitude Can Make You Happier*. New York: Houghton Mifflin.

Enright, Robert D. 2001. *Forgiveness Is a Choice: A Step-by-Step Process for Resolving Anger and Restoring Hope*. Washington, D.C.: APA Life Tools.

Ericsson, Stephanie. 2004. "How We Lie." In *50 Essays: A Portable Anthology*. Edited by Samuel Cohen. Boston: Bedford/St. Martin's.

Farkas, Steve, Jean Johnson, Ann Duffett, and Kathleen Collins. 2002. *Aggravating Circumstances: A Status Report on Rudeness in America*. Public Agenda.

Fisch, Karl, Scott McLeod, and Jeff Brenman. 2008. "Did You Know?" Video. www.youtube.com/watch?v=cL9Wu2kWwSY (accessed Feb. 19, 2010).

Fisher, Roger, and William Ury. 1981. *Getting to Yes: Negotiating Agreement without Giving In*. Boston: Houghton Mifflin.

Forni, P. M. 2002. *Choosing Civility: The Twenty-five Rules of Considerate Conduct*. New York: St. Martin's.

Franco, Zeno, and Philip Zimbardo. 2010. "The Banality of Heroism." In *The Compassionate Instinct: The Science of Human Goodness*. Edited by Dacher Keltner, Jason Marsh, and Jeremy Adam Smith. New York: W. W. Norton.

Fredrickson, Barbara L. 2009. *Positivity: Top-Notch Research Reveals the 3-to-1 Ratio That Will Change Your Life*. New York: Three Rivers Press.

Gallup. 2009. "Two in Three Americans Oppose Rep. Joe Wilson's Outburst" (20 Sept.). www.gallup.com/poll/122942/two-three-americans-oppose-rep-joe-wilson-outburst.aspx (accessed Sept. 2009).

Gilbert, Dan. 2009. "What You Don't Know Makes You Nervous." Editorial. *New York Times* (21 May).

Gladwell, Malcolm. 2005. *Blink: The Power of Thinking Without Thinking*. New York: Little, Brown.

Godin, Seth. 2008. *Tribes: We Need You to Lead Us*. New York: Portfolio.

Goleman, Daniel. 2006. *Social Intelligence: The New Science of Human Relationships*. New York: Bantam.

Guinness, Os. 2008. *A Case for Civility: And Why Our Future Depends on It.* New York: HarperOne.

Hanna, Julia. 2010. "HBS Cases: iPads, Kindles, and the Close of a Chapter in Book Publishing" (5 Apr.). *HBS Working Knowledge: Faculty Research at Harvard Business School.* http://hbswk.hbs.edu/item/6369.html (accessed Apr. 5, 2010).

Herbert, Bob. 2010. "A Recovery's Long Odds." *New York Times* (14 Sept.).

Hoffman, Eva. 1996. *Etty Hillesum: An Interrupted Life—The Diaries, 1941–1943.* New York: Henry Holt.

Intel. 2009. "Mobile Misfits Among Us: Intel Survey Reveals 9 out of 10 U.S. Adults Annoyed by Some Mobile Behaviors" (17 June). www.intel.com/pressroom/archive/releases/2009/20090617comp_sm.htm#story (accessed July 1, 2010).

Iyengar, Shanto, and Kyu Hahn. 2007. "Red Media, Blue Media: Evidence of Ideological Polarization in Media Use." Paper presented at the annual meeting of the International Communication Association, San Francisco, Calif. (23 May). www.allacademic.com/meta/p172684_index.html (accessed Apr. 16, 2010).

Johnson, Steven. 2007. "What's So Friggin' Funny?" *Discover Magazine* (19 July). http://discovermagazine.com/2007/brain/laughter (accessed July 18, 2010).

Kaplan Thaler, Linda, and Robin Koval. 2006. *The Power of Nice: How to Conquer the Business World with Kindness.* New York: Crown Business.

Kashdan, Todd. 2009. *Curious? Discover the Missing Ingredient to a Fulfilling Life.* New York: HarperCollins.

Kasson, John F. 1990. *Rudeness & Civility: Manners in Nineteenth-Century Urban America.* New York: Hill and Wang.

Keltner, Dacher. 2009. *Born to Be Good: The Science of a Meaningful Life.* New York: W. W. Norton.

Klass, Perri. 2009. "Making Room for Miss Manners Is a Parenting Basic." *New York Times* (13 Jan.).

Kosfeld, Michael. 2010. "Brain Trust." In *The Compassionate Instinct: The Science of Human Goodness.* Edited by Dacher Keltner, Jason Marsh, and Jeremy Adam Smith. New York: W. W. Norton.

Kristof, Nicholas D. 2010. "Our Basic Human Pleasures: Food, Sex and Giving." Editorial. *New York Times* (17 Jan.).

Lazare, Aaron. 2004. *On Apology.* New York: Oxford University Press.

Lenhart, Amanda. 2009. "Teens and Mobile Phones Over the Past Five Years: Pew Internet Looks Back." Pew Research Center's Internet & American Life

Project (19 Aug.). www.pewinternet.org/Reports/2009/14--Teens-and-Mobile-Phones-Data-Memo.aspx (accessed Feb. 5, 2010).

Lenhart, Amanda, Rich Ling, Scott Campbell, and Kristin Purcell. 2010. "Teens and Mobile Phones." Pew Research Center's Internet & American Life Project (20 Apr.). www.pewinternet.org/Reports/2010/Teens-and-Mobile-Phones.aspx (accessed Apr. 27, 2010).

Liljenquist, Katie, Chenbo Zhong, and Adam D. Galinsky. 2010. "The Smell of Virtue: Clean Scents Promote Reciprocity and Charity." Report: Rotman School of Management. University of Toronto. www.rotman.utoronto.ca/facbios/file/Smell%20of%20Virtue%20Psych%20Sci.pdf (accessed May 24, 2010).

Lyubomirsky, Sonja. 2008. *The How of Happiness: A New Approach to Getting the Life You Want.* New York: Penguin.

Madden, Mary, and Lee Rainie. 2010. "Adults and Cell Phone Distractions." Report: Pew Research Center (18 June). www.pewinternet.org/Reports/2010/Cell-Phone-Distractions.aspx (accessed June 28, 2010).

Marsh, Jason. 2010. "The Cost of Apathy: An Interview with Robert Reich." In *The Compassionate Instinct: The Science of Human Goodness.* Edited by Dacher Keltner, Jason Marsh, and Jeremy Adam Smith. New York: W. W. Norton.

Maxwell, John C. 2004. *Winning with People: Discover the People Principles That Work for You Every Time.* Nashville: Thomas Nelson.

Medical News. 2007. "Laughter Increases Altruism—Unselfish Concern for the Welfare of Others" (12 Mar.). www.news-medical.net/news/2007/03/12/22556.aspx (accessed July 18, 2010).

Meyer, Danny. 2006. *Setting the Table: The Transforming Power of Hospitality in Business.* New York: HarperCollins.

Mizell, Louis. 1995. "Aggressive Driving." Report: AAA Foundation for Traffic Safety (March). www.aaafoundation.org/resources/index.cfm?button=agdrtext (accessed May 9, 2011).

Modus Associates. 2010. "The Future of User-Generated Content." *Leading Edge Newsletter* (Spring). www.modusassociates.com/ideas/newsletter/spring-2010 (accessed Dec. 10, 2010).

Morrison, Terri, and Wayne A. Conway. 2004. "Getting through Customs." GetCustoms.com. www.getcustoms.com/2004XE/Articles/iw0100.html (accessed Aug. 3, 2010).

Moss, Otis, Jr. 2007. "Preface." In Stephen Garrard Post and Jill Neimark, *Why Good Things Happen to Good People: The Exciting New Research That Proves the*

Link between Doing Good and Living a Longer, Healthier, Happier Life. New York: Broadway Books.

Nielsen Wire. 2010. "Led by Facebook, Twitter, Global Time Spent on Social Media Sites Up 82% Year over Year." Weblog post (22 Jan.). http://blog.nielsen.com/nielsenwire/global/led-by-facebook-twitter-global-time-spent-on-social-media-sites-up-82-year-over-year (accessed Feb. 10, 2010).

Pearson, Christine M., and Christine Lynne Porath. 2009. *The Cost of Bad Behavior: How Incivility Is Damaging Your Business and What to Do about It*. New York: Portfolio.

Pease, Allan, and Barbara Pease. 2006. *The Definitive Book of Body Language*. New York: Bantam.

Posner, Richard Adam. 2005. "Bad News." *New York Times* (31 July).

Post, Stephen Garrard, and Jill Neimark. 2007. *Why Good Things Happen to Good People: The Exciting New Research That Proves the Link between Doing Good and Living a Longer, Healthier, Happier Life*. New York: Broadway Books.

PricewaterhouseCoopers. 2009. "Managing Tomorrow's People: Global Survey Reveals What the Millennial Generation Want from Work." (16 Feb.). www.taxtalkblog.com/?p=2219 (accessed July 18, 2009).

Provine, Robert. 2000. "The Science of Laughter." *Psychology Today* (Nov.). www.psychologytoday.com/print/22238 (accessed July 19, 2010).

PsyBlog. 2008. "Why Money Is Part of Human Nature: Money as Both Tool and Drug" (22 May). www.spring.org.uk/2008/05/why-money-is-part-of-human-nature-money.php (accessed May 12, 2010).

Purdy, Matthew. 2001. "Our Towns; After a Death, Talk Shifts from Official Ethics to Human Fairness." *New York Times* (6 May).

Radicati Group. 2009. Press Release: "Wireless Email Market, 2009–2013 Study" (Oct.). www.radicati.com/?p=4129 (accessed Mar. 5, 2010).

Radicati, Sara, and Masha Khmartseva. 2009. "Email Statistics Report, 2009–2013" (May). Radicati Group. www.radicati.com/wp/wp-content/uploads/2009/05/email-stats-report-exec-summary.pdf (accessed Mar. 5, 2010).

Rainie, Lee. 2010. "Internet, Broadband, and Cell Phone Statistics." Pew Research Center's Internet & American Life Project (5 Jan.). www.pewinternet.org/Reports/2010/Internet-broadband-and-cell-phone-statistics.aspx (accessed Feb. 5, 2010).

Rasmussen Reports. 2009. "75% Say Americans Are Getting Ruder" (22 Sept.). www.rasmussenreports.com/public_content/lifestyle/general_lifestyle/september_2009/75_say_americans_are_getting_ruder (accessed Sept. 23, 2009).

Rath, Tom. 2007. *StrengthsFinder 2.0.* New York: Gallup Press.

Reardon, Lauren. 2009. "The Radicati Group Releases 'Email Statistics Report, 2009–2013.'" Radicati Group (6 May). www.radicati.com/?p=3237 (accessed Mar. 3, 2010).

Reuters. 2010. "U.S., India Parents Seen as Worst Behaved at Kids' Sports" (7 Apr.). www.reuters.com/article/idUSTRE6364CZ20100407 (accessed May 12, 2010).

Robbennolt, Jennifer. 2010. "Apologies May Fuel Settlement of Legal Disputes, Study Says." *ScienceDaily* (3 June). www.sciencedaily.com/releases/2010/06/100602121158.htm (accessed July 9, 2010).

Rosenbloom, Stephanie. 2006. "In Certain Circles, Two Is a Crowd." *New York Times* (16 Nov.).

Sanders, Tim. 2005. *The Likeability Factor: How to Boost Your L-factor & Achieve Your Life's Dreams.* New York: Crown.

ScienceDaily. 2010. "Body's Response to Repetitive Laughter Is Similar to the Effect of Repetitive Exercise, Study Finds" (26 Apr.). www.sciencedaily.com/releases/2010/04/100426113058.htm (accessed July 18, 2010).

Seligman, Martin E. P. 1998. *Learned Optimism: How to Change Your Mind and Your Life.* New York: Pocket Books.

———. 2002. *Authentic Happiness: Using the New Positive Psychology to Realize Your Potential for Lasting Fulfillment.* New York: Free Press.

Servcorp. 2009. "Servcorp International Business Etiquette Index." Executive Suites Virtual Office Space (1 May). www.servcorp.com/media/html/ENG/Press/news_businessetiquest.htm (accessed June 22, 2009).

Simon, William H. 2005. "The Prudent Jurist." *Legal Affairs* (July/Aug.). www.legalaffairs.org/issues/July-August-2005/scene_pj_julaug05.msp (accessed Jan. 22, 2009).

Stone, Douglas, Bruce Patton, and Sheila Heen. 1999. *Difficult Conversations: How to Discuss What Matters Most.* New York: Viking.

Straker, David. 2010. "Hall's Cultural Factors." ChangingMinds.org. http://changingminds.org/explanations/culture/hall_culture.htm (accessed Aug. 3, 2010).

Sutton, Robert I. 2007. *The No Asshole Rule: Building a Civilized Workplace and Surviving One That Isn't.* New York: Warner Business.

Tapscott, Don. 2008. *Grown Up Digital: How the Net Generation Is Changing Your World.* New York: McGraw Hill.

Tavris, Carol, and Elliot Aronson. 2007. *Mistakes Were Made (But Not by Me): Why We Justify Foolish Beliefs, Bad Decisions, and Hurtful Acts.* Orlando, FL: Harcourt.

Thomas, Susan G. 2009. "Today's Tykes: Secure Kids or Rudest in History?" MSNBC (6 May). www.msnbc.msn.com/id/30585984/ns/health-kids_and_parenting (accessed May 3, 2010).

Thompson, Andrea. 2006. "Ha ha ha: Did That Make You Smile? Laughter Really Is Contagious, A New Study of the Brain Finds." MSNBC.com (12 Dec.). www.msnbc.msn.com/id/16177354 (accessed July 19, 2010).

Tierney, John. 2007. "What's So Funny? Well, Maybe Nothing." *New York Times* (13 Mar.).

———. 2008. "We Have Ways to Make You Happy." *TierneyLab Blog*, NYTimes.com (27 Mar.). http://tierneylab.blogs.nytimes.com/2008/03 (accessed July 16, 2010).

Travelocity. 2009. "2009 Rudeness Poll North America" (19 Aug.). http://i.travelpn.com.edgesuite.net/images/graphics_prod/pdf/2009_ Rudeness-Poll.pdf (accessed Feb. 18, 2009).

Tutu, Desmond. 1999. *No Future without Forgiveness.* New York: Doubleday.

University of Illinois at Urbana-Champaign. 2008. "10 Years On, High-School Social Skills Predict Better Earnings Than Test Scores." *ScienceDaily* (16 Oct.). www.sciencedaily.com/releases/2008/10/081015120749.htm (accessed Nov. 8, 2008).

University of Michigan Institute for Social Research. 2008. Press Release: "Happiness Is Rising around the World: U-M Study." University of Michigan News Service (30 June). www.ns.umich.edu/htdocs/releases/story.php?id=6629 (accessed May 14, 2010).

———. 2010. "Empathy: College Students Don't Have as Much as They Used To." University of Michigan News Service (27 May). www.ns.umich.edu/ htdocs/releases/plainstory.php?id=7724 (accessed Aug. 18, 2010).

University of Notre Dame. 2009. "What Is Generosity?" Science of Generosity Initiative. http://generosityresearch.nd.edu/about (accessed May 19, 2010).

USA Today. 2005. "We're More Rude Than We Used to Be, Americans Say" (14 Oct.).

Vascellaro, Jessica E. P. 2009. "Why Email No Longer Rules." *Wall Street Journal* (12 Oct.).

008. "Why Are the Danes So Happy? It's the Simple Things." ost (10 Aug.).

Vohs, Kathleen D., Nicole L. Mead, and Miranda R. Goode. 2008. "Merely Activating the Concept of Money Changes Personal and Interpersonal Behavior." *Current Directions in Psychological Science* (17 Mar.). www.csom.umn.edu/assets/101518.pdf (accessed May 14, 2010).

Vonnegut, Kurt. 2005. "Joe Heller." *New Yorker* (16 May).

Watson, Jason M., and David L. Strayer. 2010. "Supertaskers: Profiles in Extraordinary Multitasking Ability." *Psychonomic Bulletin & Review* (17 Apr.). www.psych.utah.edu/lab/appliedcognition/publications/supertaskers.pdf (accessed June 28, 2010).

Weber Shandwick. 2010. Press Release: "39% of American Public Tuning Out of Social Networks Due to Incivility, According to New Weber Shandwick Survey" (23 June).

———. 2011. "Civility in America." www.webershandwick.com (accessed Nov. 14, 2011).

Weir, Bill, and Sylvia Johnson. 2007. "Great Danes: The Geography of Happiness." ABC News (8 Jan.). http://abcnews.go.com/print?id=4086092 (accessed June 10, 2010).

Williams, Carla. 2007. "Is Helpfulness in Our Hormones?" ABC News (6 Nov.). http://abcnews.go.com/print?id=3827864 (accessed June 11, 2010).

Winfrey, Oprah. 2009. "Oprah on Location: The Happiest People on Earth." *The Oprah Winfrey Show* (Nov.). www.oprah.com/showinfo/Oprah-on-Location-The-Happiest-People-on-Earth (accessed May 17, 2010).

Winn, Phillip. 2008. "State of the Blogosphere: Introduction" (21 Aug.). http://technorati.com/blogging/article/state-of-the-blogosphere-introduction (accessed Mar. 3, 2010).

Zak, Paul. 2008. "The Neurobiology of Trust." *Scientific American Magazine* (June). www.neuroeconomicstudies.org/images/stories/documents/Zak-neuro-biology-of-trust.pdf (accessed May 17, 2010).

———. 2009. "The Science of Generosity." *Psychology Today* (22 Nov.). www.psychologytoday.com/blog/the-moral-molecule/200911/the-science-generosity (accessed May 17, 2010).

Zaslow, Jeffrey. 2010. "How to Prevent Verbal Gaffes." *Wall Street Journal* (7 Ju

Zhivotovskaya, Emiliya. 2008. "Smile and Others Smile with You: Health Bene Emotional Contagion, and Mimicry." *Positive Psychology News Daily* (27 S http://positivepsychologynews.com/news/emiliya-zhivotovskaya/20080927 (accessed May 25, 2009).